International Labour Organisation   **Report III**

Asian Regional Conference

Colombo, September—October 1975
Eighth Session

Third Item on the Agenda

The strengthening of labour administration in Asia and its role in national development with the active participation of employers' and workers' organisations

---

International Labour Office   Geneva

International Labour Organisation

Report III

Asian Regional Conference

Colombo, September—October 1975
Eighth Session

Third Item on the Agenda

The strengthening of labour administration in Asia and its role in national development with the active participation of employers' and workers' organisations

International Labour Office   Geneva

ISBN 92-2-101389-8

First published 1975

ILO publications can be obtained through major booksellers or ILO local offices in many countries, or direct from ILO Publications, International Labour Office, CH-1211 Geneva 22, Switzerland. A catalogue or list of new publications will be sent free of charge from the above address.

Printed by the International Labour Office, Geneva, Switzerland

TABLE OF CONTENTS

INTRODUCTION

The Governing Body of the International Labour Office, at its
193rd Session (May-June 1974), decided - as recommended by the
16th Session of the Asian Advisory Committee - to place on the
agenda of the Eighth Asian Regional Conference an item concerning:

"The strengthening of labour administration in Asia and its
role in national development with the active participation of
employers' and workers' organisations".

In recent years in Asia, there has been growing concern with
the over-all question of labour administration, as evidenced by a
series of regional and international meetings which are recalled
below.

Labour administration problems in the context of development
planning were analysed in 1969 at a regional technical round table
convened by the ILO in Manila, where it was stressed that "policy
and administration in the labour and manpower fields are as
essential" to national development "as in those, for instance,
of economics or finance".

The Seventh Asian Regional Conference (Teheran, December 1971),
when adopting a resolution concerning freedom of association for
workers' and employers' organisations and their role in social and
economic development, recommended also that "the government
ministry or department responsible for labour affairs should
wherever appropriate be the focal point for the participation of
workers' and employers' organisations in the elaboration and
implementation of development plans and programmes".

At its 15th Session (Bangkok, August 1973), the Asian
Advisory Committee, when carrying out an in-depth review of
selected programmes, including labour administration, agreed that
"the ILO could do much to help Asian labour administrations carry
out their traditional functions and also play their new role".
The Committee also "agreed on the need for intensified efforts to
make tripartite participation in all labour administration
activities more effective and meaningful".

The Fourth Conference of Asian Labour Ministers (Tokyo, 1973)
dealt with the administration of labour and manpower policies,[1]
and affirmed that it "should be given a more important status";
and the South Pacific Labour Ministers Conference (Sydney, 1973)
concluded similarly.[2]

The subject was examined on a world basis by a Meeting of
Experts on Labour Administration (Geneva, October 1973) on the
basis of a working paper[3] prepared by the ILO; the report[4]

---

[1] Fourth Asian Labour Ministers Conference, Tokyo, 1973:
Joint Communiqué, para. 5.

[2] Joint Communiqué issued by the First Conference of South
Pacific Labour Ministers (reproduced under cover of document
GB.192/21/18), para. 17.

[3] ILO: Role, functions and institutional development of
labour administration, Geneva, 1973, MELA/1973/I.

[4] ILO: Report of the Meeting of Experts on Labour Administration, Geneva, 1973, MELA/1973/V (reproduced under cover of
GB.191/9/20).

thereon recommended adopting international labour standards on labour administration.

Then, the Asian Advisory Committee at its 16th Session (Kuala Lumpur, May 1974) discussed extensively the "role and effectiveness of labour administration in Asia". The Committee concluded, inter alia, that "in connection with the formulation and implementation of national development plans, the ministry of labour needs to play a full and appropriate role. When there exists central planning machinery the ministry of labour and employers' and workers' organisations should be represented on it in accordance with national law and practice".

The Governing Body, having taken note at its 191st Session (November 1973) of the report of the 1973 Meeting of Experts on Labour Administration, decided at its 193rd Session (May-June 1974) to place on the agenda of the 61st Session of the International Labour Conference (1976) an item in respect of "Labour administration: role, functions and organisation". Finally, the Governing Body, at its 196th Session, decided to postpone this by one year. As provided for in Article 39 of the Standing Orders of the International Labour Conference, the subject will therefore come up for a double discussion by the International Labour Conference in 1977 and 1978 with a view to the adoption of international standards. The Office has, accordingly, prepared a world-wide law-and-practice report on the subject, completed by a questionnaire, which has been forwarded to governments.

The present report, which is intended for the Eighth Asian Regional Conference, is meant to bring out practical experiences in the Asian region with regard to "the strengthening of labour administration in Asia and its role in national development with the active participation of employers' and workers' organisations".

Definitions

Because of the increase in volume and variety which has occurred in the tasks performed by the State and by employers' and workers' organisations in the field of social and economic policy, there has been a development of the corresponding institutional framework and public administration machinery throughout the world, which is now so complex that the solution of certain major problems of labour policy can no longer be achieved by the "labour" ministry alone.

Generally speaking, in this report, the terms "labour ministry" or "ministry of labour" (without initial capitals) are used in a sense which is close to the expression used in article 11 of the ILO's Constitution, i.e. "the government departments of any of the Members which deal with questions of industry and employment". However, when a specific body is quoted by way of example in a particular country, it is referred to by its current name as now used in that country (with initial capitals).

On the other hand, the concept of "labour administration" - as referred to in this report - is somewhat wider and more indeterminate. The Meeting of Experts on Labour Administration (Geneva, 1973) defined it as follows:

The concept of labour administration should be interpreted in the broadest sense.

It should cover all activities by public administration bodies to assist governments in the elaboration, implementation, control and evaluation of labour policy, in the service of man.

It should cover the whole system of ministerial departments and public agencies which have been set up by national laws and regulations to deal with labour matters, and the institutional framework for the co-ordination of their respective activities and for consultation with and participation by employers and workers and their respective organisations in the formulation and development of labour policy.

Regarding the link between the notion of "labour administration" and that of "labour ministry", the same Meeting of Experts went on as follows:

The principle should be admitted that "labour administration" is not necessarily synonymous with "labour ministry".

However, measures should be taken to ensure full co-ordination for responsibilities in the field of labour policy, which, as far as is compatible with national conditions and practice, should rather be the main concern of one central body assisted by institutions for tripartite consultation and by decentralised administrative units.

Summary preview of the item before the Asian Regional Conference

What is the role of labour administration in the context of national development in Asian countries? How can its contribution to the over-all development effort be made more effective? Is there a possibility that important objectives of development may not be achieved because the potential value of the contribution of ministries of labour has been insufficiently recognised, or because their performance has been defective?

Are there any obstacles in the way of the active participation of employers' and workers' organisations in this framework? What would be the fruits of more active participation if such obstacles were removed? Which institutional devices have been experimented with that facilitate realisation of a participative approach to national objectives in the social field?

It is the practical aspects of the answers to these questions, rather than their more theoretical ones, that this report will attempt to bring out as a basis for discussion by the Regional Conference.

In doing so, the Office has been guided by the advice of the 16th Session of the Asian Advisory Committee, which made some practical points worthy of particular attention.

For instance, the following remarks are found in the Committee's Conclusions[1]:

Ministries of labour have a vital responsibility for the promotion of social progress, and their ability to fulfil this responsibility depends upon the recognition of their role by the political leadership. The labour ministry's role should be reflected in the status and authority given to it and the financial, material and staff resources made available.

The effectiveness of labour ministries is substantially influenced by the existence of strong, independent and responsible organisations of employers and workers. The participation of employers' and workers' organisations at all levels of labour administration (national, industrial, regional and local) is necessary for dynamic action by labour ministries. Adequate arrangements for such tripartite consultation and co-operation should be made.

Existing ILO standards on freedom of association and collective bargaining, labour inspection, social security and employment provide useful guidelines for national systems of labour administration.

The effectiveness of national labour administration systems depends on the existence of a central body (such as the ministry normally responsible for labour) for the formulation, implementation and co-ordination of labour and employment policies. The "central body" should also be the focal point for tripartite consultation, co-operation and participation.

Dispersal of responsibility in the field of labour policy administration may stand in the way of the integrated approach that is needed. It would make it difficult to maintain coherence between the various activities in the labour, manpower and employment field. The natural place of labour ministries in the national administration is also that of a co-ordinating "link" between the various agencies and programmes concerned with labour, manpower and employment programmes.

The basic components of the labour ministry's role in this light should be the following:

(i) administrative and technical services for establishing objectives, policies, standards, and operational programmes in relation to labour and manpower with particular reference to:

(a) full, productive and freely-chosen employment and human resources development, including training;

---

[1] Report of the 16th Session of the Asian Advisory Committee (Kuala Lumpur, 2-10 May 1974), doc. GB.193/8/16, Appendix, pp. 13 ff.

(b)   sound labour relations;

(c)   labour protection, humanisation of work and
      productivity;   and possibly

(d)   social security and welfare;

(ii)   participation in national development planning and
       plan implementation;

(iii) institutional developments in relations between
       employers and workers for both mutual and public
       advantage;   establishment and working of bipartite
       and tripartite consultation and co-operation;

(iv)   field administration in matters assigned to its
       competence according to national law and practice;

(v)   (a)   supervision of other labour administration
             agencies (statutory boards, institutes - local
             or semi-state agencies) to which specific
             responsibilities have been assigned;

       (b)   co-ordination and co-operation with other depart-
             ments in connected fields, such as education,
             health, industry, investment, trade, taxation,
             monetary policy, etc., as well as with "employer"
             departments in the public sector;

(vi)   internal administration, budgeting, accountancy,
       personnel management, staff efficiency and development,
       material resources.

Labour ministries have a particularly heavy responsibility as regards employment policy at the present time.
They should assume primary responsibility in government for
drawing the attention of all government agencies and private
institutions to the analysis and solution of employment
problems, the formulation of employment strategies and
targets, and their implementation.   While the adoption of a
comprehensive employment strategy requires the commitment and
concurrence of many agencies of government and the private
sector, labour ministries can play a key role in securing
and sustaining such commitment and concurrence.   They can
devise special programmes for utilisation of unused local
resources by employing unemployed rural labour.   In order to
assume this role ministries of labour require a new outlook,
a new competence, new attitudes and improved resources.
Further studies should be made to evaluate the experience of
member countries in this regard.

The effective extension of the role of labour ministries
is also recommended with respect to:

(i)   the rural sector in general and agriculture in
       particular (including liaison with other services
       concerned);

(ii)   (a)   the "informal" sector;

       (b)   small-scale industry;

(iii) development programmes for women's employment;

 (iv) development programmes for the employment of youth;

  (v) development programmes for the handicapped;

 (vi) collaboration with other services in matters related
       to population problems.

       In connection with the formulation and implementation of
national development plans, the ministry of labour needs to
play a full and appropriate role. When there exists
central planning machinery the ministry of labour and
employers' and workers' organisations should be represented
on it in accordance with national law and practice.

       Ministries of labour have also in this connection a
particular duty to promote equitable distribution as well as
growth of incomes, since a well-shared rising real income
is a factor of enormous impact upon production and employment.

       With regard to all the above matters, attention is
drawn to the following factors which condition the effectiveness of labour ministries:

  (i) the declared determination of government authorities
       to pursue the objective of social progress with full
       respect for freedom of association and collective
       bargaining;

 (ii) the political will to establish a more just society,
       to share out the nation's wealth more equitably, to
       give workers and employers more say in the relevant
       functions of government;

(iii) the whole state of public administration of a country
       conditions the efficiency and efficacy of its labour
       ministry;

 (iv) equally the efficacy and efficiency of employers' and
       workers' organisations in influencing policies and
       programmes and their implementation in the context of
       national development are also reflected in the labour
       ministry;

  (v) there has to be a will to pursue labour and manpower
       policies which reach beyond the modern sector;

 (vi) the character of the labour problems encountered must
       be fully understood and met with resources adequate
       for their solution;

(vii) labour legislation should be sufficiently evolved,
       updated and adjusted to meet all operational require-
       ments and international commitments.

Ministries of labour should have available the necessary resources (including statistical and research and planning services, staffed by competent and well-trained officials) to make correct diagnoses of the country's socio-economic needs, to put forward the right options applying the proper priorities, and to contribute effectively to a clear statement of policy objectives. The adequacy of their informational and statistical base should be reviewed from time to time and if necessary upgraded.

Status, career development and promotion prospects of labour ministry staff should be commensurate with the importance of the responsibilities and duties that they have to discharge.

On this basis, the text of this report has been organised as follows:

Chapter I briefly records some background information about the existing framework of labour administration in Asia. It refers to the responsibilities of the services concerned regarding the formulation and implementation of labour policy in relation to developmental aims, and gives country examples of such responsibilities, together with details of the administrative machinery, in respect of employment matters, training, income and conditions of work and life, labour-management relations and aspects of social security and welfare. It describes particularly the arrangements for participation by employers' and workers' organisations of various countries in the functioning of these services and mentions how certain services help to develop new targets in the labour, manpower and employment fields. Examples are then given of the institutional framework and administrative procedures through which some Asian ministries of labour take part in development planning, including the use of tripartite and bipartite consultation in this process.

Chapter II discusses various problem areas in the role and operation of labour administration agencies in Asia and also notes a number of suggestions for possible solutions. The more general aspects of scope of responsibility are first discussed, and newer areas of action in the fields of employment and training, conditions of work and life, and labour relations, are reviewed. Then the means for more significant participation by employers' and workers' organisations in labour administration activities are considered. This is followed by consideration of measures for increasing the effectiveness of ministries of labour, and by observations regarding international technical co-operation in this sphere.

To facilitate the discussions of the Conference, a list of suggested points for discussion has been added.

CHAPTER I

ORIENTATION OF LABOUR ADMINISTRATION IN ASIA

Part A: Responsibilities of Asian labour
         administration agencies regarding both
         formulation and implementation of
         labour policy in the light of
         development targets

General remarks

The traditional role of labour administration

The governmental units responsible for labour affairs, in
their early traditional roles, were development agencies only in
the sense that they helped improve working conditions for a
relatively small proportion of the labour force by preparing and
enforcing laws and regulations concerning hours of work, minimum
rates of pay and safety of workers and by regulating labour-
management relations.

As these activities developed, labour administration agencies
became involved in other functions as well. They dealt, for
instance, with the settlement of disputes between workers and
employers, at first perhaps informally and later, as experience
developed, within an institutional and legislative framework.
Then, as organisations of workers and employers became more
widespread and gained official recognition, some labour administration agencies were also given the responsibility of enforcing
legislation concerning the registration and activities of unions
of workers and employers. They also, in some countries, became
the agencies which administered schemes for compensating
employees who were injured at the workplace.

These early roles of securing compliance with labour legislation, regulating conditions of employment, and promoting sound
relations between employers and workers still represent a large
proportion of the work of virtually all ministries of labour in
the region, and in some countries they are by far their pre-
dominant area of concern.

Involvement in the provision of employment exchanges and vocational training

By the early 1950s, however, two other areas of activity had
become important responsibilities of a number of labour administration agencies in Asia. Firstly, with the growth of the
organised sector, there was an increased demand for wage or
salary earners, particularly those with skills and training, and
labour ministries became involved in setting up employment
exchanges designed to bring together workers who were seeking jobs
and employers who were seeking labour. Secondly, they had become
involved in vocational training by applying legislation, such as

apprenticeship laws, prescribing the obligations of employers and workers who entered into contracts to give or receive vocational training. In some countries labour ministries had also taken on the additional role of actually providing vocational training - to a smaller or larger degree - through their own institutions.

By this stage, therefore, such labour ministries had become important agencies in implementing plans to provide enterprises with the workers they needed.

Providing planners with basic data on employment trends

It was on reaching this stage that some labour administration agencies found they could make a significant contribution to formulating manpower and employment policies, as well as implementing them. In operating their employment services, for instance, they collected statistics on unemployment by sex, age, region and occupation which when compiled and processed gave valuable information on the availability of surplus manpower. Employment exchanges also collected statistics from employers on unfilled vacancies and labour shortages and this information provided a useful base on which vocational training plans could be formulated. Information which they collected on wage rates and earnings was useful in planning industrial development policies. Furthermore, through their various services and contacts with employers and workers, they collected a substantial amount of unquantifiable information on the state of the labour market which could usefully be taken into consideration in the formulation of manpower plans.

Such information, particularly that relating to skill shortages, was much sought after by planners who had begun to appreciate the importance of obtaining an adequate supply of skilled and trained workers to provide the industrial production on which further development was to be based.

There developed, therefore, in a number of countries a limited working relationship between the central planning ministry and the labour ministry with regard to the preparation of the manpower section of the national plan. The labour ministry would supply the planning ministry with whatever useful information it possessed on manpower trends and problems. The planning ministry would then amalgamate this with other data received from other agencies, analyse it, and formulate manpower and employment policies.

Involvement in the formulation of manpower and employment policies

Although it would not be correct to assume that in most countries of Asia ministries of labour at that stage engaged in any in-depth manpower/employment policy formulation, they began to realise that their role in this regard could be further widened and improved. For instance, recognising the shortcomings for planning purposes of the statistics they collected in the normal course of operating employment exchanges, they began undertaking separate surveys to provide them with information which they would not otherwise obtain. Some Asian labour ministries, for example, began to undertake sample surveys to identify unemployment or underemployment which was not known to employment exchanges but which nevertheless needed to be taken into account when formulating plans to create additional jobs. Other ministries of labour, in addition to compiling statistics on current vacancies reported to employment exchanges, began undertaking area skills surveys to identify skills which would be needed in the future and for which vocational training would have to be planned.

A further development was that, in addition to providing the planning agency with more comprehensive information, some labour administration services began to analyse it and provide policy advice. For instance, as well as providing the planning ministry with basic statistics on unemployment, they are now giving advice on the types of employment which need to be created. They have also, as a result of their growing expertise in economic matters and their long experience in industrial relations, given policy advice on such matters as redundancy and how to avoid it.

Some ministries of labour have increased their involvement in manpower planning to the point where they now play a key role in preparing detailed policy plans to bring about a balance between the supply of, and demand for, labour throughout the organised sector. Such policy advice has proved valuable to planners in that it comes from an agency which has close day-to-day contact with employers and workers, combined with an intimate knowledge of industry. In the exercise of this task, a better understanding of the necessity of co-ordination with ministries of education is also coming about.

This increased activity in planning has, in turn, enabled such ministries of labour to increase the effectiveness of some of their other services. As their knowledge of the future needs of the economy increases, so does the value of the advice given through their employment exchanges. In some cases, too, labour administration agencies, through their analyses of labour supply and demand, have established advisory services to inform employers about which geographical areas are most likely to be able to provide the type of labour they need. The competence and prestige acquired in this respect also benefit the services which deal with labour relations and labour protection.

Further development of roles in formulating and implementing labour policies

There is today a growing realisation that a strong case can be made for extending still further the planning functions of ministries of labour, and perhaps also the functions of some of their operational services. It is recognised that in order to achieve over-all economic and social goals, it is necessary to take into account the entire labour force and not merely those who work in the organised sectors or in the urban areas. This is particularly the case in countries where workers are moving from the rural areas to the urban centres to find work, or where the rural labour force is of great importance to the dynamic progress of the country.

It is also recognised that at the present time many ministries of labour are for the most part concerned only with the activities of the organised sector of the labour force, which in many Asian countries represents less than 20 per cent of the total number of workers. Consequently, labour administrators in these countries feel that they are handicapped by lack of knowledge of what is happening in the rural sector and they have even found that policy advice given for one sector may conflict with, or adversely affect, decisions in others. It is true that, in isolated cases, there have been comprehensive employment plans for the rural sector, the plans being prepared by the ministries of planning and agriculture. Frequently, however, in these cases both the labour ministry and the ministry of agriculture communicat independently with the planning ministry, and there is little direct communication between them as yet, although signs of closer co-operation have begun to appear.

Added to this is the fact that the technical quality of employment planning, and the emphasis which is placed on manpower matters, can vary considerably. Labour administrators, by virtue of their functions and responsibilities, have a fuller apprecia- tion than most officials in other agencies of the importance of manpower development for achieving suitably balanced social and economic development. In their policy advice to the planning ministry, they tend to give high priority not only to using labour productively but also to improving working conditions. This might not be the case with employment plans prepared by other agencies, since the latter's main preoccupation tends to be economic growth, and manpower is apt to be considered as a means to achieve this end rather than as a factor to be developed in itself.

It is therefore necessary to devise administrative systems which ensure that the total labour force is given the priority and prominence it deserves in economic and social planning, and which also ensure that the manpower planning activities of different agencies are well co-ordinated.

The question remains to what extent it is necessary, desirable or practicable to extend the role and jurisdiction of the labour administration system so that it has responsibilities and functions relating to the entire labour force in all sectors and all geographical areas.

The 16th Session of the Asian Advisory Committee - as pointed out in the Introduction - was of the view that ministries of labour should assume a particularly important responsibility as regards employment policy, and that they should assume a primary role in government "for drawing the attention of other state agencies and private institutions to the analysis and solution of employment problems, the formulation of employment strategies and targets, and their implementation". Although the adoption of a comprehensive employment strategy requires the concurrence of many agencies of government, it was the view of the Asian Advisory Committee that a ministry of labour should play an important part in securing and sustaining such concurrence. In regard to employment creation, the Committee considered that ministries of labour needed to give fuller attention to the rural sector and to the development of special programmes for women, youth and handicapped persons.

The 1973 Meeting of Experts on Labour Administration had also been unanimously of the view that there was scope for defining a much more active role for ministries of labour in the formulation and development of long-term national employment problems and in the field of training and placement services. In this respect, the Experts' Meeting came to the conclusion that labour ministries had a continuing responsibility to persuade other public agencies operating in the fields of economic policy, agricultural and industrial development, population, education, taxation, trade, public investment and other related matters, of the over-riding importance of employment objectives; that close consultation and collaboration by ministries of labour with representative organisations of employers and workers was necessary at all stages in the formulation and development of employment policies; that ministries of labour should have available the major elements of information and evaluation to be taken into account in the elaboration of short-term employment policies and emergency measures aimed at countering unemployment, under-employment and maladjustments of the manpower situation; that the implementation of employment policies, both long-term and short-term, as well as their evaluation were areas in which the services of ministries of labour were indispensable; and that labour administration services should assist also in implementing a government's population policy, especially in countries where this was a major factor in the present and future employment and well-being of workers.

In this connection it is also interesting to note that at the Fifth Conference of Asian Labour Ministers (Melbourne, April 1975) the panel which discussed the agenda items concerning the economic and social aspects of employment promotion was of the view that "the success of employment policies depends largely on the effectiveness of government agencies concerned with labour administration. This in turn emphasises the value of programmes aimed at improving the organisational structure and work methods and developing the personnel of labour administrations. National employment services and labour market information systems particularly must be effective for manpower programmes to be successful. International agencies can assist in this area by providing fellowships and material and technical assistance".

Responsibilities with respect to employment and training

As pointed out above, the span of employment problems is so wide that activities related to the elaboration, implementation and evaluation of a national employment policy aimed at achieving full, productive and freely chosen employment go well beyond the range of action of labour administration, but they tend to involve the latter more and more. In many Asian countries, the appropriate institutional framework for performance of these activities is still being developed, and many Asian labour administration agencies are now actively involved or are considering a more active involvement.

As responsibilities in this broad area of policy are shared, in all countries, between various departments of government, a better understanding is emerging of their respective contributions and of the need for co-ordination in this area.

At the same time, the concept of a comprehensive employment policy has been developed. It has been fairly generally accepted in Asia that employment policy (as envisaged by the Employment Policy Recommendation, 1964, No. 122) should be co-ordinated with, and carried out within the framework of, over-all economic and social policy, including economic planning or programming in countries where such instruments are used. Moreover, it is recognised that the solution of employment problems clearly figures among the objectives of development, and does not just arise from economic growth. Indeed, solution of certain employment problems can be seen as an essential prerequisite of development.

This understanding of a comprehensive employment policy has helped to put in a clearer light the relevance and correlations of three approaches already in existence, each being related to a distinct conceptual premise, but complementary to the others in practice. It may be useful to recall them.

The manpower planning approach consists mainly in the balancing of present and foreseeable manpower supply and demand, and is related to the planning of education and training.

The employment planning approach aims beyond this stage and seeks to orient the plan towards employment objectives, from which sectoral target rates of growth are then derived; in this process an economic policy choice is implied.

The employment promotion approach aims at giving practical effect (in various fields) to the two above-mentioned types of planning, particularly in rural areas which may be more severely handicapped by economic and social imbalances.

Examples of this evolution are numerous in Asia. Virtually all the governments have, either through their national plans or through explicit or implicit policy statements, made full and productive employment a target of national socio-economic policy. In some Asian countries, there is no longer a lack of declared intentions or of theoretical knowledge on how to pursue a full and productive employment policy; more often, there are infrastructural shortcomings or severe difficulties in practical organisation and implementation which prevent these countries from maintaining a steadier balance between supply and demand for labour.

It is important that the types and extent of imbalances on the labour market are known, that their causes are analysed and that countervailing measures are taken both to initiate structural changes - laid down in national plans - as well as to deal with shorter-term imbalances.

In several Asian countries, governments have clearly defined the aims of employment policy, and certain instruments have been devised. For instance, in Australia, the Government pursues as a major goal an active policy designed to promote full, productive and freely chosen employment. Full employment is a permanent aim of economic policy, based on endorsement by successive Australian Governments of the original White Paper issued in 1945, which laid down that "Full employment is a fundamental aim of the Commonwealth Government. The Government believes that the people of Australia will demand and are entitled to expect full employment", and that "Governments should accept the responsibility of stimulating spending on goods and services to the extent necessary to sustain full employment". In this country, responsibility for employment policy in its practical execution is regarded as being divided essentially between the labour and the economic ministries.

In Japan the arrangements give joint charge of the formulation of employment policy to the ministry responsible for labour questions and the planning body. The Ministry of Labour works out a state master plan for employment (at the request of the Cabinet). This plan is drafted on the basis of discussions between the Minister of Labour and the heads of the administrative agencies concerned, while the views of the Employment Council and prefectural governors are also obtained. The master plan clarifies the various employment problems from the standpoint of manpower prospects and establishes the future basic direction of employment measures and necessary policies. Harmony with the over-all state plan for the economy is also a requirement. The Ministry of Labour then works out, in compliance with the plan, an annual employment programme which it implements. It is also responsible for employment administration throughout the nation, by giving guidance to the prefectural governments in their elaboration of master and annual employment plans in conformity with the state plan.

India and Malaysia have accumulated a considerable degree of experience in economic and social development planning, with high priority being devoted to manpower development. Both countries, moreover, have appreciated that labour administration agencies can play an important role in helping to utilise manpower resources fully and improve working conditions. They have therefore increased in recent years the involvement of their ministries of labour in the formulation and implementation of manpower plans, and there is widespread recognition that further improvements and a deeper involvement can still be achieved.

In the Philippines there has been a growing acceptance of the need to give higher priority to employment generation and manpower development in national economic and social development planning. This has been due largely to the initiative and sustained effort of the Department of Labour. Over recent years, the Department has been involved increasingly in development planning and employment/manpower policy formulation. The National Manpower and Youth Council is responsible for initiating and co-ordinating manpower policies and programmes. The Council, which is attached to the Department of Labour for policy and programme co-ordination, is composed of most of the Cabinet members and the Director-General of the National Economic and Development Authority. The Council Secretariat consists of an office of manpower planning and development, a national manpower skills centre, and regional manpower development centres. The Secretariat of the Council has, inter alia, the following functions and responsibilities: (i) to prepare and recommend the manpower plan for approval by the Council; (ii) to recommend allocation of resources for the implementation of the manpower plan as approved by the Council, and (iii) to prepare for approval by the Council an annual report to the President on plans, programmes and projects on manpower and out-of-school youth development. The Council is also responsible for vocational training and skill standards.

In Thailand the Government has recently approved the creation of a national manpower council of which the Department of Labour is a member. The council is expected to study manpower and employment problems and to recommend policies and programmes which will help to resolve these problems in line with the national development plan.

In Sri Lanka, the Ministry of Planning and Economic Affairs has the major responsibility in the area of manpower planning and skill development. However, there is, at present, a growing realisation that the labour ministry could and certainly should have a more active role, and a review of the employment/manpower machinery in the ministry is under consideration.

The labour administration system in the USSR places great emphasis on effective utilisation of manpower through "scientific organisation of work". This is the responsibility of the State Labour and Wages Committee of the Council of Ministers of the USSR. The Committee has, among its five major departments, a department for the organisation of labour and the fixing of norms, which operates through the offices for labour and wages in the various industrial ministries. Distribution of manpower and its absorption into employment is governed by other specialised bodies of the State. All these processes are closely planned and subject to final governmental approval. The central planning machinery has counterparts in the constituent republics. Associated with the structure are the ministries for each sector of economic activity, the state committees (ministries) for vocational training and technical education and for co-ordination of research and scientific work. There is the closest liaison throughout with the vast organisation of the Central Council of Trade Unions.

In several other Asian countries, ministries of labour play an important role in contributing to the definition of the general employment measures which need to be taken, even where the execution of most of these general employment measures is outside their direct responsibility.

Most Asian ministries of labour, however, have responsibilities for the drawing up and implementation of short-term or selective employment measures, while - being often the secretariat to employment councils - they also contribute to the co-ordination of general and selective employment measures.

Examples of the devising and implementation of selective employment measures are found throughout Asian ministries of labour. For instance in Indonesia, the Ministry of Manpower is responsible for the transmigration scheme of workers and their families from Java to the outer islands. Internal migration is also financially and otherwise assisted by the ministries of labour in for example Australia, Japan and New Zealand. In Fiji, Pakistan and the Philippines, the ministries of labour assist workers in finding work overseas, while in Australia and New Zealand, the labour ministries assist foreign workers in settling down properly. In Iran, the Department of Employment within the Ministry of Labour has, inter alia, the functions of (i) ascertaining short and long-term employment opportunities in the country; (ii) assisting in drawing up short-term programmes for overcoming urgent problems and situations connected with manpower; and (iii) participating and assisting in drawing up and implementing plans for employing graduates of the institutions

of higher education.   Several other important employment
responsibilities for many Asian ministries of labour include
aspects of labour market information, placement, vocational
training, employment counselling, vocational guidance, which will
be dealt with later in this chapter.

Employment information

Whereas the Employment Policy Convention, 1964 (No. 122)[1]
provides that employment policy "shall take due account of the
stage and level of economic development and the mutual relation-
ships between employment objectives and other economic and social
objectives, and shall be pursued by methods that are appropriate
to national conditions and practices" (Article 1); the Employment
Policy Recommendation, 1964 (No. 122) deals more specifically with
the need for employment information.   Paragraph 4(1) provides
that "employment policy should be based on analytical studies of
the present and future size and distribution of the labour force,
employment, unemployment and underemployment".

This need has been recognised in Asian countries and employment market information is being collected from different sources
both within and outside ministries of labour.

An important source for detecting structural changes in the
employment market is provided by national censuses, which are for
instance taken by the central statistical offices once every
five years in Australia and New Zealand and once every ten years
in India, Indonesia, Pakistan and Singapore.   This information -
which often becomes available only after periods of two to three
years from its date of collection - is being supplemented by
employment data collected through sample surveys or annual
censuses of industry.

For instance, in India labour force surveys are conducted
annually while in Pakistan this is done quarterly and in Japan on
a monthly basis.   In Thailand such surveys are conducted from
time to time.   Censuses of industry also provide some employment
information in Australia, for instance, where an annual census
of some sectors of industry such as manufacturing and mining is
conducted.

Another source of employment information in Asian countries
consists of the registration of job applicants and the notification of vacancies with employment service offices.   It is through
this method that, for example, in Australia the Commonwealth
Employment Service of the Department of Labour and Immigration
collects information on a monthly basis on the numbers of unemployed
applicants and unfilled vacancies, according to various categories,
occupations and industries.   In Japan, India and Malaysia and
several other Asian countries, also, the employment services
provide detailed employment information.

---

[1] This Convention has been ratified by the following countries
of the region: Australia, Iran, Khmer Republic, Thailand, USSR
and Viet-Nam.   The Convention was included among those selected
for review by the Asian Advisory Committee and Asian Regional
Conference in 1970 and 1971, as it was considered to be relevant
to the priority needs and the economic and social realities of
the region.

The coverage of the data, as well as their reliability, however, differs from one country to another. Generally speaking, in developing countries the changes in the employment situation are measured most frequently for the modern and industrialised sector, while the rural areas are not often included in the data. In the more developed countries, a wider coverage is achieved, on account of the higher intensity of wage and salary employment. For instance, in New Zealand the Department of Labour carries out an employment information survey twice a year (in mid-April and mid-October) which covers firms employing two or more persons in all sectors except farming, fishing, hunting, waterfront and seagoing work, domestic service in private household and armed services, and this accounts for about 75 to 80 per cent of full-time employees and obtains information on numbers employed, hours worked and wages paid.

The institutional agency responsible for employment information collection differs according to the purpose of the exercise. Responsibility for censuses naturally belongs to census bureaux in the various central statistical offices. Labour force sample surveys are sometimes taken by ministries of labour, as for instance in Singapore, sometimes by other agencies such as the National Sample Survey Organisation in India and the National Statistical Office in the Philippines and Thailand. Finally, the employment services of ministries of labour in countries like Australia, Japan and New Zealand play a key role in obtaining current employment market information. In other Asian countries, this role is less pronounced but still very important, as for instance in India and Malaysia.

Once the employment information has been collected it needs to be analysed and interpreted. This function is carried out by the labour ministries in Australia, Japan and New Zealand, India, Malaysia, the Philippines and Singapore. Sometimes for this purpose a special labour market information service is established, as for instance in the Ministry of Labour and Manpower of Malaysia.

If important employment problems necessitate special analysis, some ministries of labour carry out ad hoc studies. This is done for instance by the ministries of labour in India, Malaysia and the Philippines. The manpower survey of May 1973 carried out by the Ministry of Labour and Manpower of Malaysia, for instance, was designed to provide nation-wide information in order to: (a) assess the educational and skill attainments of those at present employed in various occupations; (b) assess the extent of current shortages of trained personnel by occupations; (c) assess the extent of on-the-job training undertaken by the private sector and the use of outputs from vocational training institutions; (d) project future manpower requirements by occupations to enable better planning of education and training programmes.

The system used for the collection of information is sometimes highly technical. In Japan, for instance, the Labour Market Centre of the Employment Security Bureau of the Ministry of Labour operates a network of data transmission circuits and large electronic computers which integrate and process the various data transmitted from the public employment security offices. In Malaysia also a central computer is used and each office, having sent in key characteristics of job registrants and of those placed, receives back every month an analysed tabulation of its figures.

Placement

Part of the functions of employment services in Asian countries is to facilitate placement, either locally or abroad, and to provide advice to job seekers on the kind of jobs which would be most suitable for them, taking into account the opportunities on the employment market.

Most employment services in Asia register applicants and take note of their occupational qualifications, experience and desires and interview them for employment. Sometimes different types of registration exist for different types of workers. In Japan, for instance, the public employment security offices are divided - depending on the form of employment - into a general employment service, a simplified employment service (for part-time workers) and a labour employment service (for day labourers). Notifications of vacancies are received from employers either compulsorily or voluntarily. There is an obligation to notify vacancies for instance in India, and Pakistan, while in most other Asian countries, a voluntary system of notification is in operation.

Placement arrangements for special categories of occupations are also made in some countries. For instance in India a central employment service has been set up to deal with job vacancies of a scientific and technical nature, and in Japan special "talent banks" exist at public employment security offices for assisting persons with technical and managerial skills. In Fiji a special register of professional technical and managerial staff is maintained.

Arrangements for placements beyond the limits of the local area exist in several Asian employment systems, for instance in Australia, Japan, the Philippines and Sri Lanka. In Japan, this wider area placement operates through the above-mentioned integrated data processing system at the Labour Market Centre of the Ministry of Labour. In Sri Lanka, the Central Employment Exchange in Colombo carries out the placement function in respect of any excess of job vacancies and job seekers for the provinces under its "clearing-house" procedure.

A special kind of advisory and placement service is rendered by the employment service in Malaysia, besides its normal placement service. It assists prospective employers well ahead of the commencement of production by assessing their labour requirements by occupation and the appropriate plant location from the point of view of labour supply.

Overseas employment arrangements are part of the placement functions of some Asian employment offices, for instance in Fiji and the Philippines. In Fiji, the recently established employment service in the Ministry of Labour is responsible for arranging the supply of labour under the New Zealand Employment Scheme, whereby local unskilled workers are sent to New Zealand for temporary employment of up to four months. In the Philippines, an overseas employment development board has been constituted for the recruitment of Philippine nationals who want to work overseas, and a national seamen's board has been created which provides training and placement and seeks the best possible conditions for seamen. The Secretary of Labour is chairman of both boards.

Fee-charging placement offices exist in some Asian countries, but are under forms of regulation and control by ministries of labour. In Japan, for instance, these agencies are allowed to operate for 26 specified categories of workers including artists, but are subject to control. In the Philippines, the Labour Code of 1974 provides that all fee-charging employment placement agencies must be phased out by 1978.

Vocational guidance and counselling

Vocational guidance and counselling are part of the services provided in several Asian countries by employment offices. The objective of providing such services is to assist the job seeker in making a vocational choice more in line with his capabilities or to help him to assess which occupations are open to him and how he could adjust his skills so that more desirable occupations would suit him.

The vocational guidance and counselling service is mostly concentrated on certain (potential) groups of workers such as youth, handicapped persons, older workers and certain other special groups.

For youth, in Australia for instance, the Commonwealth Department of Labour contributes, during the period that the child is still at school, to educational and careers guidance by providing information about occupations and the labour market. In Pakistan, vocational guidance officers have been posted in regional employment exchanges in certain important areas. One of their main functions - besides giving general employment counsel - is to visit educational institutions and impart vocational guidance to students. In India, special university employment and guidance bureaux have been established at 52 universities, while the recently established Career Study Centre within the Central Institute for Research and Training in employment service compiles and publishes careers literature, which is distributed free of charge to all schools and educational institutions.

Older workers receive special attention from employment offices, for instance, in Japan where the public employment security offices have special "older persons' corners" for providing detailed guidance and counsel to this class of workers.

Handicapped workers also get special support from several Asian ministries of labour, sometimes in terms of vocational counselling and guidance, sometimes through retraining at the labour ministry's vocational rehabilitation centres, as in Japan. In that country, agricultural workers also receive specialised guidance by the newly established employment offices in rural areas of Japan.

In India, a special type of guidance and placement-cum-training programme is carried out by the employment service in respect of applicants belonging to "scheduled castes" and "scheduled tribes" who register at the service, through special centres whose function is to equip those job seekers with the necessary skills to enable them to face various types of tests and interviews held by the Government and other public bodies.

Training

Training standards are maintained and institutionalised in several Asian countries, but the arrangements for vocational training and trade testing follow different patterns among them. Some Asian countries have also made arrangements for the retraining of skilled workers at an older age.

In some of the countries persistent efforts are made to co-ordinate vocational training according to an integrated vocational training plan, prepared and executed in collaboration between several agencies, including the ministry of labour and sometimes also employers' and workers' organisations.

For instance in Australia a national employment and training system has been introduced in 1974, which supersedes previous training schemes. The new system, known as NEAT, has six broad objectives: (i) to alleviate unemployment and its effects by providing training opportunities for retrenched workers, disadvantaged job seekers and persons faced with declining opportunities in relation to employment potential - and paying them while they learn new skills; (ii) to widen the range of skills of the Australian labour force; (iii) to increase the ranks of skilled workers; (iv) to assist in the long-term reconstruction and redeployment of the labour force; (v) to promote regional development of industries; (vi) to serve the social as well as the economic needs of the community and individuals by means of special assistance, guidance, remedial training and other measures to aid removal of inequalities and enhance employment opportunities.

In Japan the Ministry of Labour's first five-year basic vocational training plan became operational in 1971 and has since been implemented. The plan aims at the realisation of a system of lifetime training under which workers can receive appropriate vocational training at any stage in their working lives and seek to: (i) triple the number of school graduates given basic training; (ii) double the number of employed workers taking adult vocational training; and (iii) expand the trade skills tests to cover 200 types of trades, and to this end, actively implement the necessary measures. Each prefecture draws up similar plans for its territory.

In Mongolia a national industrial training scheme has also been established. Within this scheme a unified system of vocational training, including in-plant training, has been adopted.

In the Philippines the new Labour Code prescribes that the National Manpower and Youth Council, which is attached to the Department of Labour for policy and programme co-ordination, is responsible for the formulation of a long-term national manpower plan for the optimum allocation, development and utilisation of manpower.

Apprenticeship schemes exist in the majority of Asian countries, as for instance in Australia, India, New Zealand, Pakistan, the Philippines and Singapore.

The administrative agency responsible for the operation of
the scheme is practically always the ministry of labour or a
connected agency. For instance in Australia the Departments of
Labour of the States predominantly carry this responsibility,
while the Commonwealth Department of Labour and Immigration
administers apprenticeship training in its own special field.
In Singapore it is the Industrial Training Board, on which the
Ministry of Labour is represented, that has apprenticeship
training among its responsibilities.

Approval for entering into apprenticeship agreements is
sometimes a responsibility of the ministry of labour. For
instance in the Philippines the Secretary of Labour approves the
trades and occupations in which enterprises may engage workers
under apprenticeship agreements.

Expenditure on apprenticeship training is sometimes tax
deductable or is financially supported by the ministry of labour,
as for instance in Australia, Japan, New Zealand and the
Philippines.

In addition to apprenticeship, skills are also imparted in
many Asian countries through formal training at vocational
institutes. The agency responsible for this type of training
is sometimes the ministry of labour, as for instance in Bangladesh
India, Japan, Mongolia (State Committee for Labour and Wages),
Pakistan, the Philippines, Sri Lanka and Thailand. The
responsibility covers the standards of qualifications of persons
eligible for public vocational training facilities, the subject
matter of training, the duration of training, the equipment
required, etc.

In some cases there are also various private training
centres, particularly in Japan, where quality standards are
supervised by the ministry of labour and financial assistance
is sometimes rendered to these centres.

In Pakistan, the provincial labour departments are
responsible for the institutional type of training; in Japan
the Ministry of Labour, the prefectures and the Employment
Promotion Projects Corporation share the public responsibility
for it; and in the Philippines the responsibility rests with
the above-mentioned National Manpower and Youth Council, which
is attached to the Department of Labour for policy guidance
and co-ordination.

Generally speaking, craftsman training is provided at
industrial training institutes. The differences between Asian
countries lie mainly in the type of skills trained for, the
number and quality of training instructors and the number and
quality of training institutes.

In Japan and various other Asian countries, advanced and
instructor training are distinct from ordinary craftsmen training.
In India, for instance, for advanced levels of training there are
three institutes: (i) Foremen Training Institute in Bangalore
for the training of foremen and supervisors; (ii) the Advanced
Training Institute in Madras for the (master) craftsmen, and
(iii) the Central Staff Training and Research Institute in
Calcutta for training of training officers from industry in the
control and management of training programmes. There are
similar technical institutions in New Zealand.

Certain vocational training centres for special groups of workers also exist. In India, for instance, there are four vocational training institutes catering specially for women, to assist absorption into industry. In addition to handicrafts training by established training institutes, more mobile units are in use in Sri Lanka and Thailand.

Notes on administrative machinery

The above-mentioned functions of Asian labour ministries in the fields of employment and training involve use of a network of employment exchange offices, training institutes, etc., under the direction and co-ordination of central and regional units. In this section some examples are given of such machinery.

The basic operational machinery, for instance, in Australia, consists of the Commonwealth Employment Service (160 full-time offices, 329 agents and 1 part-time branch) and various technical education institutions. The employment offices fall directly under the responsibility of the Commonwealth Department of Labour and Immigration, which also has vocational guidance units staffed by psychologists and clerical support personnel located in each capital city (there are two in Melbourne), and in Darwin, Townsville and Launceston. The latter units are functionally responsible to the chief psychologist, Applied Psychology Section of the Central Office, and administratively to the regional directors.

In Bangladesh there are five employment exchanges, five technical training centres for vocational training, three apprenticeship training offices and four youth employment offices.

In India there are 515 employment exchanges, 357 industrial training institutes for the training of craftsmen, 7 craft instructor training institutes, 2 advanced training and 1 central staff training and research institutes, and 6 vocational rehabilitation centres. There are also 218 vocational guidance units set up at employment exchanges. The employment exchanges depend for financing on the respective states in which they are established. The Central Ministry of Labour (Directorate-General of Employment and Training) is responsible for laying down policy, standards and procedures for uniform adoption all over India.

In Japan the Ministry of Labour has at its disposal 481 public employment offices, a labour market centre, 442 vocational training centres giving basic training, an employment promotion projects corporation at the Occupational Research Institute, talent banks, vocational centres for the physically handicapped, terminal employment counselling centres and part-time work "corners" for special classes of job applicants. In this country, the responsibility for the functioning of the public employment security offices is shared between the Ministry of Labour and the prefectural employment security sections. Employment security councils, composed of equal representation of labour, management and public interests, are organised on the national and prefectural levels and in special areas where dockworkers are numerous.

In Malaysia, the employment service has a network of 30 full-time and 31 part-time offices and has been reorganised as a separate unit within the Manpower Department of the Ministry of Labour and Manpower, which also supervises training institutes.

In Mongolia there are 13 vocational schools which are under the direct supervision of local industrial enterprises, but the responsibility for the technical organisation rests with the State Committee for Labour and Wages, in which the Department of Vocational Training is located. There are plans to increase the number of schools, while a pilot training centre for the accelerated training of instructors, supervisors and skilled workers has already been established at Ulan Bator.

In New Zealand, the Department of Labour provides, through its 21 district offices, employment information, counselling and placement services. The Education Department administers a vocational guidance service for young persons.

In Pakistan there are six technical training centres and 28 employment exchanges. Two more technical training centres and one apprentice training centre are being set up during 1974-75. Also in existence is an apprenticeship training scheme.

In the Philippines there are 39 employment offices spread out over the islands under the responsibility of the Department of Labour.

In Sri Lanka the employment service of the Department of Labour is operated through 36 employment exchanges and 58 registration centres functioning in different districts and divisions of the island.

In Thailand the Department of Labour directly supervises five employment exchange offices, while the provincial labour offices under the administrative authority of provincial governors also carry out employment service functions. In this country, also under the aegis of the Department of Labour, the National Institute for Skill Development has been operating since 1969. Three regional multi-purpose skill development centres are being established. Some 50 mobile trade training units offer skill training to persons in remote areas.

Apart from this basic machinery, mention should be made of the special arrangements to deal at a higher level with such matters.

In Australia, for instance, in the matter of apprenticeship training, co-operation between the Commonwealth and State Departments of Labour has led to the establishment of the Australian Apprenticeship Advisory Committee (AAAC). The Committee meets annually and comprises the permanent heads of State Departments of Labour, Directors of Technical Education and the executive of each state's apprenticeship authority (or their representatives)

together with representatives of the Apprenticeship and the
Technical Education Authorities of the Commonwealth Department
of Labour.   AAAC recommendations have contributed to Australian
government initiatives to promote apprenticeship in a number of
ways.

Other standards of vocational training have also been given
attention in Australia.   This led to the establishment in 1971
of a tripartite National Steering Committee on Training for
Industry and Commerce (now named the National Training Council).
It was formed to advise the Minister for Labour on the development
of training in Australia, to encourage the assessment of
occupational training needs on an industry-by-industry basis and
to promote the appointment of skills training officers to enterprises and to industry associations.   Some tripartite Industry
Training Committees have already been established to conduct
surveys of manpower training needs in their industry and to
implement the recommendations resulting from these surveys.

In Hong Kong the Industrial Training Advisory Committee
provides the Government with advice on major industrial training
questions.   The Commissioner of Labour is ex officio chairman
of this Committee.   The Committee on Vocational Training is
also chaired by an official of the Labour Department.

In Malaysia the need was felt in 1970 for improving the co-
ordination and intégration of all programmes of industrial training.   A Co-ordinating Committee on Employment and Training was
accordingly established, replacing the Subcommittee on Employment
and Training of the National Operations Council.   In the newly
established committee, all ministries and departments involved
in all kinds of training are represented.   In addition to this,
a National Industrial Training and Trade Certification Board
(NITTCB) exists in Malaysia, for which the Training Service of
the Manpower Department of the Malaysian Ministry of Labour and
Manpower provides the secretariat.   Its functions are to:
(i) establish national standards of industrial training and
trade certification; (ii) define the roles of the agencies
concerned with training for industry and assist them in raising
their standards of training and in increasing their output;
(iii) launch an extensive in-service training programme organised
within industrial establishments themselves; and (iv) train
trades instructors for both the public and private sectors to
assist in overcoming principal bottlenecks in the implementation
of training programmes.   In order to provide liaison between the
NITTCB and the various branches of industry and employer and
worker groups, the National Advisory Council on Industrial
Training was established.   Two areas of main concern to the
Council are: (i) assessment of manpower requirements; and
(ii) a National In-plant Training Programme.

In New Zealand, in order to assist employers in planning
and carrying out vocational training in their own establishments,

the Department of Labour has an Industrial Training Service, which provides specialist training services to industry. In order to provide for better co-ordination in forecasting needs and to recommend programmes to meet these needs, a Vocational Training Council was established in 1968 under the administrative control of the Education Department. Representative industrial and commercial training boards have been formed in some 25 industries. Each includes members from employer, employee, educational and other specialist groups. These boards among other tasks examine existing training and assess the need for revised or new schemes. This involves both the identification of the level of ability of the person required (machine operator, graduate, tradesman, supervisor, etc.) and the numbers required at each level. Very close liaison is maintained between the Department of Labour and the Vocational Training Council and Industrial Training Boards.

Responsibilities with respect to income and conditions of work and life

This is the area of labour administration activities which has perhaps the longest tradition in many Asian countries.

The Asian Round Table on Labour Administration and Development Planning (Manila, 1969) pointed out that in approaching the subject of developmental labour administration, there was a danger to be guarded against, namely of seeing it as something wholly new replacing what had been done in the past. There are, however, in this regard also, important matters with respect to which ministries of labour can undertake developmental functions. They can assist, for instance, in identifying social and human factors which it is necessary to include in integrated socio-economic policies, and in associating employers' and workers' organisations with various forms of action aimed at the improvement of incomes and conditions of work and life. Furthermore, it is still the case that in several Asian countries the bulk of the rural population outside plantations remains beyond the protection of most labour laws, and that even in the industrial and commercial sectors, this sometimes applies to workers in smaller enterprises (e.g. those employing less than ten workers). In the more developed industries, rapid technological changes are bringing about the need for newer forms of protection; preoccupation with the environment is growing, as is concern in certain countries over income security in the face of economic fluctuations, or a better relationship between conditions of life and conditions of work.

Awareness of many of these factors is clearly evident in a number of recent statements on labour policy, as in, for instance, Indonesia, Japan, Pakistan and the Philippines.

General conditions of work, occupational safety and health inspection

The basic administrative means of applying legal provisions on labour protection has of course been labour and factory inspection, which exists in virtually all Asian countries.

The subject is regulated by the Labour Inspection Convention, 1947 (No. 81) which, as at 31 March 1975, had been ratified by Bangladesh, India, Japan, Malaysia, New Zealand, Pakistan, Singapore, Sri Lanka and Viet-Nam, and by the Labour Inspection (Agriculture) Convention, 1969 (No. 129)[1] which, as of 31 March 1975, had been ratified by no Asian country.

A report submitted to the 14th Session of the Asian Advisory Committee (Bandung, 1970) pointed out that, among obstacles to ratification of Convention No. 81 in certain countries, there were obstacles of a legal nature, which stemmed from the fact that the provisions of national legislation, although frequently analogous in substance to the Convention, were far less specific than the latter, especially as regards the powers and obligations of inspectors. These difficulties were by no means peculiar to Asian countries, and the Committee of Experts noted that they were of a technical nature and did not appear to be due to any objection of principle on the part of governments to the provisions of the Convention.[2]

Another type of difficulty arises in some countries from additional duties (i.e. duties extraneous to the functions related to law enforcement) which are sometimes entrusted to the labour inspection service, especially duties in the field of labour relations. In several Asian countries, significant efforts have been undertaken to organise these functions more efficiently on a distinct basis, as in the cases of Hong Kong, India, Japan, Malaysia, etc.

Complex difficulties of a practical nature arise from the co-ordination of labour inspection services whenever they are split in different branches (some outside the control of the

---

[1] These Conventions were included among those selected for review by the Asian Advisory Committee and the Asian Regional Conference in 1970 and 1971 as they were considered to be relevant to the priority needs and the economic and social realities of the region.

[2] See: AAC/XIV/II, Problems encountered in the ratification and application of selected Conventions, ILO, Geneva, 1970, p. 55.

ministry of labour, as is the case of factory inspection in
Thailand) and for the solution for which some countries have
preferred to regroup them under one head.   Even more serious
difficulties are encountered when different departments of
government contest the ministry of labour's right of labour
inspection in sectors of economic activity under their more or
less direct purview.

Roughly speaking, the basic organisation is founded on a
general labour inspectorate in, for instance, Japan and the
Philippines, while separate general labour inspectorates and
factories inspectorates operate for instance in Australia,
Bangladesh, India, New Zealand, Pakistan and Sri Lanka.   In
the USSR labour inspection is carried out not only by public
officials but also by trade unions, co-ordination being achieved
at the level of the State Committee for Labour and Wages Questions
of the Council of Ministries of the USSR, and the All-Union
Central Council of Trade Unions.

In a large number of countries the labour administration
agencies suffer in varying degrees from an insufficiency of
resources, and in some countries, indeed, the administration
exists only in embryo.   The labour inspection service, in
particular, is not always in a position to act effectively,
and is handicapped, inter alia, by lack of staff - due partly
to poor conditions of service - and of facilities.

It may be noted in this connection that the Labour Inspection (Agriculture) Convention, 1969 (No. 129) suggests in
Article 8(2) that "so far as it is compatible with national
laws or regulations or with national practice, Members may
include in their system of labour inspection in agriculture
officials or representatives of occupational organisations, whose
activities would supplement those of the inspection staff;   the
persons concerned shall be assured of stability of tenure and
be independent of improper external influences".

With regard to the inspectorates' capacity in the crucial
area of occupational safety and health, many are handicapped
not only by shortage of staff, which reduces their ability to
supervise adequately the implementation of the relevant national
legislation and to keep abreast with rapid technological
developments, but also by lack of resources for research and
transfer of knowledge in this area.   None the less, distinguished
examples of research institutes can be quoted, as in the cases,
for instance, of India, Japan or the USSR.

Wages

While in some Asian countries wage levels for some categories
of workers are determined unilaterally by employer decisions, in
other cases they are established through collective bargaining
or through statutory minimum wage-fixing machinery.   The
ministries of labour may be involved in this field of protection
in several ways.   Many of them, as in Bangladesh for instance,

calculate, often in co-operation with the Bureau of Statistics, a cost-of-living index for the working population in different areas, which is utilised in wage negotiation or other forms of wage determination or adjustment.

The responsibility of a great number of Asian ministries of labour includes, in general, the setting and supervision of minimum wages, either through decisions by tripartite wages boards or on the advice of such boards. This matter is the subject of three international labour Conventions. Of these the Minimum Wage-Fixing Machinery Convention, 1928 (No. 26) has been ratified by Burma, India, Japan, Sri Lanka and Viet-Nam; the Minimum Wage-Fixing Machinery (Agriculture) Convention, 1951 (No. 99) by the Philippines and Sri Lanka; and the Minimum Wage-Fixing Convention, 1970 (No. 131) by Australia, Japan, Nepal and Sri Lanka.

At the national level, as for instance in Bangladesh, a Minimum Wages Board is empowered to prescribe minimum wages, and has in practice done so, particularly for establishments employing 50 workers or less.

Nepal also has a Minimum Wage Board which fixes minimum wages. In Sri Lanka there are now 32 such boards for the various trades, while minima for employees are laid down by ten Remuneration Tribunals.

In other Asian countries it is the ministries of labour which fix minimum wages, and in various cases do so in agreement with the views of wages boards. In Afghanistan it is the Ministry of Mines and Industry - in which the Labour Department is located - that establishes minimum wages for industrial workers. In India minimum wages have been fixed and revised for the scheduled industries in accordance with the Minimum Wages Act of 1948. In Japan, minimum wages can be established along two lines - either by collective agreement, or based on the views submitted to the Ministry of Labour or prefectural bureaux by the Central or Prefectural Minimum Wages Councils. In certain cases, Japan's trade unions and employers may ask the Minister of Labour or the Chief of the Prefectural Labour Standards Bureau to determine, amend or abolish the minimum wages as established by collective agreement. The Minister or Chief of the Prefectural Bureau can in such cases ask the Minimum Wages Council for advice. In the Philippines, the Tripartite Wages Commission recommends the Secretary of Labour to make minimum wage orders in industry as a whole or various branches. In Thailand, the Department of Labour has responsibility for establishing statutory minimum wages after consultation with the Wage Board.

Different systems exist in other countries. In Indonesia, for instance, a Presidential Decision of 1969 established a

national wages research board under the aegis of the Ministry of
Manpower. Its terms of reference are to advise the Government
on wages policy in the short and long term, bearing in mind the
economic and manpower factors concerned and economic development
in the broad sense of the term. All relevant ministries, the
central bank, BAPPENAS (i.e. the central planning body) and
representatives of employers' and workers' organisations are
members of this board, which is chaired by the Minister for
Manpower. By a ministerial decision of 1970, provision was
made for the setting up of regional wages boards under the
chairmanship of the respective provincial governors in some
provinces.

Australia and New Zealand form a distinct case. In
Australia, the federal tribunals (arbitration tribunals and
wages boards) are empowered to make awards under the Conciliation
and Arbitration Act. The respective states' industrial
tribunals have corresponding tasks for their areas of responsibility. Similar machinery exists in New Zealand.

The implementation of minimum wages orders and the provision
of the secretariat to wages boards are ensured by the ministry of
labour in practically all Asian countries. The implementation
of the awards made by tribunals in Australia and New Zealand is
also ensured by central and state labour inspectorates.

Special advisory assistance in this field has been provided
in Japan. The ministry of labour of this country started in
1967 a "system of wage consultants" under which a "wage consultation corner" has been established in all the prefectural labour
standards bureaux and major local labour inspection offices (of
which there are 56). The consultants provide advice, assistance
and guidance to employers and workers for the improvement of
their systems of wage calculation.

Ministries of labour and social
security administration

The role played by ministries of labour in the implementation
of social security schemes differs from one Asian country to
another and even within the one and same country, according to
the different types of social security measures adopted.

For example, the risk of employment injury, i.e. industrial
accidents and occupational diseases, had been originally covered
by a scheme based on the principle of individual employer's
liability for the payment of compensation (usually called a
workmen's compensation scheme). The provisions of such schemes
are usually enforced through the machinery of the labour (or
workmen's compensation) commissioners in the ministry of labour,
as in Bangladesh, Burma, India, Malaysia, Pakistan, Singapore and
Thailand.

In some of those countries, however, a social insurance
scheme has already been introduced to cover the same risk, and
where an employer is covered by the scheme, he is relieved of
the statutory obligations under the employer's liability scheme.

In such a case the role played by the ministry of labour in the administration changes to a considerable extent in that the daily operation of the social insurance scheme is entrusted by law to an institution set up exclusively for the administration of the scheme.

Such an institution is in some cases a department of the ministry of labour. For example, the social insurance scheme covering employment injury is directly run by the ministry of labour in Japan and Thailand. In other countries such as Burma, India, Iran, Malaysia and Pakistan, an independent institution of a public corporate nature is set up to administer the scheme, and it is important to note that the governing body of such an institution is tripartite in its structure, having employers' and workers' members together with the government representatives. However, the institution is usually under the general supervision of the Minister responsible for labour affairs in those countries.

Similar observations can be made concerning other risks such as sickness and maternity, in respect of which individual employers were originally made responsible for the provision of benefits, but subsequently a social insurance scheme was introduced.

It should, however, be noted that the social insurance scheme which has been introduced in many developing countries of Asia is still limited in its scope of application, and substantial numbers of wage earners and salaried employees even in the organised sector are still under the protection extended by the employer's liability scheme in the contingency concerned. This means that the ministry responsible for labour affairs is directly in charge of administration of the law establishing such a liability in a given contingency, whereas in respect of the persons covered by a social insurance scheme dealing with the same contingency, an independent statutory institution is responsible for the administrative operation, with the exception of countries where the social security scheme for workers is directly administered by a government department.

As for long-term contingencies such as old age, invalidity and death of the breadwinner (of non-occupational origin) there is no employer's liability scheme in the countries of Asia. In some countries such contingencies are covered by a provident fund scheme on a statutory basis. The scheme is administered by a public body, as in the case of social insurance, for example in India, Malaysia and Singapore, where the ministry of labour is responsible for a general supervision of the actual administration by such a body. In Sri Lanka, the provident fund scheme is administered jointly by the Department of Labour and the Central Bank of the country. Such contingencies are covered by a social insurance scheme in Iran, Philippines and Japan. The scheme in the first two countries is also administered by a public body whereas different pension schemes of Japan are directly managed by government departments concerned.

The following table indicates social security institutions administering schemes in selected countries of Asia under general supervision by the government in respect of different contingencies:

	Contingencies covered	
	Sickness, maternity, employment injury	Old age, invalidity, death
Burma	Social Security Board	-
India	Employees' State Insurance Corporation	Employees' Provident Fund
Iran	Social Insurance Organisation	
Malaysia	Social Security Organisation[1]	Employees' Provident Fund
Pakistan	Provincial Employees' Social Security Institutions	-
Philippines	Social Security System[2]	
Singapore	-	Central Provident Fund

[1] Employment injury only, but it also administers a scheme of invalidity pension (non-occupational origin).

[2] Maternity not covered.   Employment injury to be covered soon.

Welfare administration in labour matters

Workers' welfare is one of the responsibilities of nearly all Asian ministries of labour.   It ranges from questions relating to welfare and amenities within the establishment to certain welfare facilities for workers outside the establishment.

This report in this subsection restricts itself to certain aspects of these questions such as the help provided by labour administration in the fields of population policy, workers' housing and welfare (for instance in plantations), property accumulation by workers, welfare services for migrant workers, and the like.

In certain Asian countries ministries of labour are increasingly being requested to assist in the application of population policies where workers in the organised sector are concerned.   The Asian Symposium on Labour and Population Policies (Kuala Lumpur, August 1972) highlighted the role of the

ministry of labour in this respect. The Symposium found[1],
inter alia, that "the organised sector programme should envisage
a pivotal role for the labour administrations since they have
constant dialogue with employers' and workers' organisations on
such matters as labour welfare, social security, occupational
health and workers' education. The labour administration should
facilitate the review and co-ordination of the family planning
programme in the organised sector by the national family planning
organisation and make the necessary arrangements to this end".
The Symposium concluded that "labour administration should
(i) integrate family planning education with the schemes of labour
educational programmes arranged for workers, so that these workers
can in future act as effective educators/motivators among their
colleagues; (ii) undertake family planning education of persons
covered by social security schemes where the scheme has a health
care component through group and individual contacts. Consideration should be given to how other branches of social security can
contribute to information and educational aspects of family
planning and the promotion of the small family norm; (iii) broaden
the scope of occupational health services to cover family planning
activities".

Effect has been given to several of these recommendations.
For instance in India the Ministry of Labour is represented on the
newly established Tripartite National Committee on Family Welfare
Planning. Furthermore, the Employees' State Insurance Corporation and the Coal Mines Welfare Fund under the central Ministry of
Labour play also an important part in that programme. The Central
Board of Workers' Education has of late been engaging fairly
actively in imparting motivation and instruction in family planning
through the agency of its 36 regional centres spread throughout
the country. In Sri Lanka's Ministry of Labour there is a special
unit established to provide educational programmes in family
planning to both urban and estate sectors. The Ministry has
established tripartite committees at the national, regional,
district and estate level under the chairmanship of labour ministry
officials, in order to support workers' education on family
planning matters.

In the matter of workers' housing, some Asian labour ministries
have taken up responsibilities for the establishment and enforcement of standards with respect to the housing provided by employers
to the workers. This has been particularly significant in cases
where fairly large concentrations of workers occur, for instance
in countries where the plantation sector is widespread as in
Bangladesh, India, Pakistan, Sri Lanka and Malaysia, or at mining
sites, etc.

Sometimes workers' housing is promoted through the use of
funds accumulated under social security schemes or through
specially established welfare funds. The latter is the case in
Pakistan, where employees can contribute to a workers' welfare
fund for the financing of housing schemes. In India, the Coal
Mines Welfare Fund has also partially been supporting workers'
housing. In Singapore, the contributions to the Provident Fund
Scheme may be used as the basis for receiving a low-interest loan
from the Housing and Development Board for buying a low-cost

---

[1] Report on the Asian Symposium on Labour and Population
Policies (ILO/ECAFE, 1972).

appartment. Finally, in Japan the Minister of Labour decides,
on the basis of recommendations by the tripartite Council of
Workers' Property Accumulation, on policy with regard to this
workers' property accumulation scheme.

Other welfare services - for instance on plantations - are
also sometimes supervised by labour administration services,
e.g. the protection of the rights of workers' children and other
benefits to which workers' families are entitled under labour
laws.

With regard to welfare services for migrant workers, the
departments of labour in Australia and New Zealand, for instance,
carry out special responsibilities. In New Zealand, the
Employment and Immigration Division of the Department of Labour
maintains work camps and 11 hostels accommodating over 1,200
persons, including coal miners, migrants in seasonal industries
and immigrants who have not made prior arrangements for permanent
housing and need temporary lodging. In Australia, the Department of Labour has recently also been made responsible for
immigration. In addition to its responsibilities for work
permits, it arranges in a similar fashion for the receipt of
immigrant workers.

Responsibilities with respect to labour relations

Several Asian countries have laid down rules and procedures
for the registration of trade unions.[1] Registration of trade
unions is, for instance, carried out by the state labour departments in Australia, by the Ministry of Labour's Directorate of
Trade Union Registration in Bangladesh, by the State and Central
Labour Commissioners in India, by the Director of Industrial
Relations of the Ministry of Manpower in Indonesia, by the state
labour departments and the National Industrial Relations
Commission in Pakistan, by the Commissioner of Labour in
Sri Lanka and by the central and provincial registration offices
in Thailand.

This registration is for some countries compulsory, as in
Hong Kong, Iran, Malaysia, Singapore and Sri Lanka. In other
countries it is optional, but a prerequisite for acquiring
certain rights.

According to the labour legislation of several Asian
countries, an appeal may be lodged against the administrative
decision on registration. In Malaysia and Singapore for instance
the appellate instance is the minister for labour.

Rules for the selection of the most representative union
are included in the legislation of several Asian countries.
For instance in Australia the Registrar must, unless in the
circumstances he thinks it undesirable to do so, refuse to
register any organisation if another organisation to which the

---

[1] For a more in-depth treatment of this matter, one may
refer to the report on Freedom of association for workers' and
employers' organisations and their role in social and economic
development, Report III to the Seventh Asian Regional
Conference, ILO, Geneva, 1971.

members of the former might "conveniently belong" has already
been registered. Similar legislation has been enacted in the
States of the Commonwealth.

Restrictions on the election of outsiders as trade union
representatives exist in several Asian countries, but for instance
in Sri Lanka, the minister of labour may waive the requirement
that at least 50 per cent of a trade union's officers must be
engaged in the industry concerned.

Ministries of labour of several Asian countries are
responsible for the implementation of the legislation concerning
the protection of workers against acts of anti-union discrimina-
tion. This is for instance the case in Australia, Japan,
Malaysia, Pakistan, the Philippines and Singapore.

Under the legislation of most Asian countries, trade unions
enjoy the right to bargain collectively, and many Asian labour
ministries have adopted an active policy to promote collective
bargaining and protect the right to bargain collectively.
A report submitted to the Seventh Asian Regional Conference[1]
pointed out some of the methods employed to implement such a
policy, e.g. the establishment of a procedure for the recognition
of trade unions (by employers) as collective bargaining
representatives; the device of making the unjustified refusal
of an employer to bargain collectively with the representative
of his employees subject to the procedure for the prevention of
unfair labour practices; and the use of government conciliation
services not only for settling disputes but also to encourage
and assist collective bargaining and to promote voluntary
methods of settling disputes.

Statutory provisions dealing with the recognition of trade
unions by employers are enforced by several Asian ministries of
labour, for instance in some States in India, in Indonesia,
Japan, Malaysia, Pakistan, the Philippines and Singapore.

Asian ministries of labour are mainly involved in labour-
management relations at times when employers and workers are
deadlocked, but may even be called in to settle procedural
disputes between the two groups.

Many Asian ministries of labour have a conciliation service
which attempts to mediate between the two parties. For instance,
in Indonesia the procedure for the settlement of labour disputes
is that where the parties to an unsettled dispute do not intend
to make use of the arbitration procedure, the fact must be
notified to the Director of Industrial Relations at the Ministry
of Manpower, Transmigration and Co-operatives or to the
industrial relations official at the regional or ressort office.
Such notification is regarded as a request to intervene by way
of conciliation. A similar procedure exists in Thailand.

In Sri Lanka the Commissioner of Labour or an authorised
officer appointed by him makes the conciliation attempt.

---

[1] Freedom of association for workers' and employers'
organisations and their role in social and economic development,
Seventh Asian Regional Conference, Report III, ILO, Geneva,
1971, p. 25.

In some other Asian countries conciliation is sought through tripartite bodies.

In New Zealand the Conciliation Council will attempt to reconcile the parties, after labour inspectors of the Industrial Relations Division of the Department of Labour or of the district offices have investigated the work disturbances and stoppages.

If conciliation or mediation efforts are unsuccessful, then different ways are open, depending on the country concerned, some of which may imply tasks for the labour administration machinery.

One way is through voluntary arbitration. In Bangladesh, for instance, one of the tasks of a conciliator is to persuade the parties, when it comes to this, to submit their dispute to an arbitrator. In India the Labour Commissioners and other authorised labour officers can refer to the Code of Discipline in Industry and the Industrial Truce Resolution adopted voluntarily by the central organisations of employers and workers, which includes voluntary arbitration as one of the methods for solving disputes. In Malaysia, reference can also be made by the labour officers to such a code of discipline. In Thailand, if after a conciliation attempt by the labour department officials the parties still fail to agree, then voluntary arbitration may be undertaken by one or three independent labour dispute arbitrators, to be agreed upon by the parties concerned.

In Australia and New Zealand compulsory arbitration is part of a system of industrial relations which has functioned for over 70 years. In Indonesia, the Regional Committee for the Settlement of Disputes makes recommendations to the parties, which the parties may accept or reject. In the latter case the Committee is empowered to make binding decisions, but an appeal may be lodged with the Central Committee and its decision is binding if the Minister for Manpower does not nullify it or postpone its execution.

In the Philippines labour arbiters have to decide cases within 45 days when a deadlock has occurred, but an appeal can be made to the National Labour Relations Commission. The Commission's decision can only be reversed by the President, on the proposal of the Secretary of Labour, in the national interest.

Another way, for labour conciliation officers to solve a dispute in some Asian countries - after all conciliation efforts have failed - is to refer the dispute to adjudication bodies. For instance, in India there is a three-tier adjudication system - Labour Courts, Industrial Tribunals and National Industrial Tribunals. In Malaysia, an Industrial Court hands down awards. In Pakistan, Labour Courts at the zonal level and Labour Appellate Tribunals at the provincial level adjudicate upon industrial disputes, while a National Industrial Relations Commission determines industrial disputes at industry and national level. In Sri Lanka, in cases of deadlock in collective bargaining, the Industrial Courts decide, while Labour Tribunals deal with individual complaints.

Many labour ministries in Asian countries have in recent years emphasised the preventive and educative role they can play in

labour-management relations.[1]   For instance, in Burma the Office
of the Central Committee on Industrial Arbitration within the
Ministry of Labour is responsible for ensuring that township labour
arbitration committees are constituted.   In India, as in other
Asian countries, ministries of labour have supported the creation
of bipartite consultation bodies like Works Committees, Joint
Management Councils, etc.   In Japan the desire for prevention of
disputes has led to the establishment of the Industry and Labour
Council where regular meetings are held between the Prime Minister
and top leaders of employers' and workers' organisations; and in
Pakistan the National Industrial Relations Commission has, inter
alia, as functions: to promote trade unions and to advise the
Government on the workers' education plan.

In some Asian countries ministries of labour assist directly
the educational efforts of employers' and workers' organisations
and are promoting the establishment of responsible organisations
of employers and workers.

For instance, in Bangladesh the Industrial Relations Institute,
under the aegis of the Ministry of Labour and Social Welfare, has
been carrying out a series of courses for trade union leaders,
government officials and management officials.   In Iran, the
Ministry of Labour and Social Affairs has been implementing the
Literacy Programme since 1971, which has as its objective to
educate one million workers over an eight-year period.

Part B: Participation by employers' and
          workers' organisations in the function-
          ing of Asian labour administration systems

In most Asian countries, governments and particularly labour
ministries, generally seek the advice of employers' and workers'
organisations on major labour policy matters, including changes in
labour legislation.

The type of formal and informal arrangements made for seeking
the views of employers' and workers' organisations differ from one
country to another or according to the object of consultation.[2]
The frequency of the consultations differs also.   Some of the
arrangements have already been mentioned.   This chapter describes
some further examples.

---

[1] The Fifth Asian Regional Conference (Melbourne, 1962) discussed the subject of "Government services for the improvement of
labour-management relations and settlement of labour disputes".

[2] The establishment of national bodies with responsibilities
for the implementation of ILO standards has been the subject of an
agenda item at the 60th (1975) Session of the International Labour
Conference: National tripartite machinery to promote implementation of ILO standards, International Labour Conference, 60th Session,
1975, Report VII(1) and (2).

<u>Administrative arrangements for the
participation of employers' and workers'
organisations in Asian labour
administration systems</u>

In Australia, regular consultations between the Government and
representatives of employers and workers are a normal procedure.
This may cover any aspect of labour and related policies and indeed
much of the general business of government. The consultations have
taken the form of ad hoc talks or representations reinforced by
regular, formal meetings of established machinery and regular discussions, e.g. the annual pre-budget discussions. A National
Labour Advisory Council, with members drawn from the central
organisations of employers and workers, was set up in 1968 to
provide a forum for regular tripartite consultation on employment,
industrial relations and related industrial and economic matters.
The NLAC set up two committees to advise on the impact of
technological change and on aspects of women's employment in
Australia. Tripartite bodies with broadly similar functions
related to the responsibilities of State Labour Departments have
been set up in several States. Furthermore, most of the States
have an apprenticeship authority, usually attached to the State's
Labour Department. Organisations of employers and workers are
represented on this authority. At national level, there is the
Australian Apprenticeship Advisory Committee, also tripartite in
character. Tripartite industry training committees are also
established.

In Bangladesh employers and workers are associated in the
formulation of the Government's labour policies through participation in the Labour Advisory Board and various other tripartite
bodies. In the judicial sphere, the labour courts consist of a
chairman who is a senior judicial officer and two members, one to
represent the employers and the other to represent the workers.

In Burma the Social Security Board consists of 17 members of
which the Minister of Labour is ex officio chairman, with four
other ex officio members (one from the labour ministry) and six
worker and six employer representatives. Day-to-day operations
are managed by a standing committee, also tripartite, under the
Director of Labour.

In Fiji, in fields of major administration where boards and
committees are set up by the Government, the workers and employers
are represented. One of these organisations is the Labour Advisory
Board, which examines legislation affecting workers that is to be
introduced by the Government. Although the Board acts in an
advisory capacity, the matters raised in the meetings of the Board
either by the workers' representatives or the employers' representatives are given due consideration by the Government. Some other
statutory bodies on which both sides of industry are represented are
the Fiji National Provident Fund, National Economic Council, Fiji
National Training Council, Fiji Council of Industrial Relations and
the Manpower Resources Council. Informal consultations also take
place with workers' and employers' organisations.

In India, the central tripartite consultative machinery comprises mainly the Indian Labour Conference and the Standing Labour
Committee, on which representatives of employers' and workers'
organisations sit along with representatives of central and state

governments to consider labour policy from time to time. Besides
these bodies there are also tripartite industrial committees which
have been set up to consider the specific problems of labour
employed in individual industries like cotton textiles, jute
textiles, iron and steel, chemicals, mines, plantations, etc.
With regard to employment and training in India, there exist the
tripartite Central Committee on Employment, the tripartite National
Council for Training in Vocational Trades and the Central Apprenticeship Council. Another specialised tripartite body is the Central
Implementation and Evaluation Committee which deals with matters
relating to the implementation of the Code of Discipline for labour-
management relations and effective implementation of labour law,
etc. Also, a tripartite Committee on Conventions periodically
reviews the position with regard to the ratification of ILO Conventions and the application of international labour standards.
Most of the state governments have also constituted tripartite
bodies at the state level. The Minimum Wages Advisory Boards are
also tripartite, and so are the Dock Labour Boards and the Dock
Workers Advisory Committee. Other statutory bodies of a tripartite
character are the Standing Committee of the Employees' State
Insurance Corporation; the Central Board of Trustees set up under
the Employees' Provident Funds and Family Pension Funds Act; the
Board of Trustees of the Coal Mines Provident Fund Scheme; and the
Tripartite Advisory Committees of the Mica Labour Welfare Fund, the
Coal Mines Labour Welfare Fund and the Iron Ore Mines Labour Welfare
Fund.

In Indonesia employers' and workers' organisations nominate
representatives to serve on the Central Committee for the Settlement of Labour Disputes, and also representatives to serve on the
related regional committees. The National Wages Research Board
and the Regional Wages Boards are also tripartite.

In Iran consultation with workers' and employers' organisations
takes place through various means. One of them is the Tripartite
National Labour Conference, which is held each year before the
International Labour Conference. In addition, there is the
Central Training Council, in which general training programmes and
policies are drawn up. Other examples are the Central Labour
Council, which has, inter alia, the function of approving the
regulations for application of the Labour Code; the Central Social
Insurance Council, which is inter alia responsible for approving
the regulations concerning social security legislation; and the
Central Safety Council which approves the regulations for occupational safety.

In Japan the opinions of employers and workers and the public
interest are reflected through statutorily and non-statutorily
established bodies. At national level, there is the Industry and
Labour Council, which is composed of members representing workers
and employers, persons of knowledge and experience and members
representing the Government; it meets every month to exchange
views with regard to industrial labour policy. Other more
specialised tripartite statutory bodies in Japan are the Central
Labour Standards Council, the Women's and Minors' Problems Council,
the Central Employment Security Council, the Central Vocational
Training Council, the Central Minimum Wages Council, the Smaller
Enterprise Retirement Allowance Mutual Aid Council, the
Pneumoconiosis Council, the Central Industrial Home Work Council,

the Workmen's Accident Compensation Council, the Council for Workers' Property Accumulation, and the Physically Handicapped Persons' Employment Council. With regard to quasi-judicial functions in labour-management relations, a tripartite Central Labour Relations Commission exists as well as tripartite Local Labour Relations Commissions.

At prefectural level, there are also the tripartite prefectural Industrial and Labour Councils, the tripartite statutory prefectural Employment Security Councils, the tripartite prefectural Labour Standards Councils, etc. Finally, since February 1974, the "Administration Consultation Room", which was set up on the Labour Ministry's secretariat to receive opinions from the public concerning the working of labour administration agencies, has been expanded with the creation of the "Labour Ministry's Post 1313" through which any citizen can express his opinions or desires about labour administration.

In Malaysia the labour administration has a close working relationship with labour and management at national level through the National Joint Labour Advisory Council and its committees. The Council is a tripartite advisory body comprising governmental, employers' and workers' representatives. The Minister of Labour and Manpower is the Chairman of the Council. The function of the Council is to advise the Minister on: (a) questions affecting labour and promotion of industrial peace; (b) matters in which employers and workers have a common interest; and (c) ways and means to stimulate regular consideration of matters within the purview of the Council. Apart from that country's National Joint Labour Advisory Council, representatives of employers and workers are appointed to sit in various bodies connected with labour administration such as (i) wages councils; (ii) the Social Security Board; (iii) the National Industrial Training and Trade Certification Board; (iv) the National Advisory Council on Industrial Training; (v) the Port Labour Board; (vi) the National Electricity Board; (vii) the Malaysian Railways Board; (viii) the Employees' Provident Fund Board; (ix) the South Indian Labour Fund Board and the Malaysian Migration Fund Board.

In Nepal a tripartite central Labour Advisory Board was appointed with the following terms of reference: "There shall be established a Labour Advisory Board at the centre to assist in the formulation of labour policies. The Board shall be at liberty to deliberate and recommend on any matter affecting labour in general and in particular questions relating to industrial relations, labour legislation, employment and productivity". Another tripartite body, the Minimum Wage Board, was established by the Government under the Factory and Factory Workers Act to "deliberate on unduly low wages referred to it and make recommendations for the fixing of statutory minimum wages for any category of workers". The head of the Department of Labour is secretary-cum-member of both boards and the staff of the Department carries out the ground work for all items placed on the agenda for discussion.

In New Zealand the 1973 Industrial Relations Act established a tripartite industrial relations council which serves as an advisory body to the Government on all industrial relations matters. Furthermore, recently a tripartite vocational training council was established which in turn established sectoral industrial training boards. The functions of the council are advisory to the Government and its departments, and to industry, commerce, agriculture, social welfare and other interested organisations in the field of industrial training. The 22 industrial training boards examine, among other things, existing training arrangements and assess the needs for revised or new schemes.

In Pakistan a tripartite labour conference and the Standing Labour Committee at the national level, and the labour advisory boards at the provincial level provide forums for eliciting the views of labour and management for the formulation of government policies. The National Industrial Relations Commission is tripartite in composition and so are the wages boards and the governing bodies of social security and workers' welfare funds. Other bodies exist which have tripartite composition and perform specific administrative or quasi-judicial functions.

In the Philippines the 1974 Labour Code established a national labour relations commission and as many regional branches as necessary, each headed by a labour arbiter. The National Labour Relations Commission is headed by a chairman representing the public, two members representing the workers and two members representing the employers. The chairman and the members are appointed by the President, as well as the labour arbiters of the regional branches. Additionally, the Social Security Commission is a tripartite body composed of the Secretary of Labour, the Social Security System Administrator and six appointed members, two of them from labour, two from management and two representing the general public. Tripartite conferences and consultative meetings are also held from time to time on subjects related to labour.

In Singapore there are informal meetings and discussions whereby the views 'of labour and management are sought and presented to labour ministry officials. At the more formal level, management and labour representatives sit on the board of directors of important statutory bodies. Thus the National Wages Council, the Central Provident Fund Board and the National Productivity Board are tripartite.

In Thailand the Wages Board is tripartite and ad hoc wages committees have been established by provincial governors for advising on minimum wage rates for each of the 71 provinces. Finally, a labour relations commission has been established on which employers and workers are also represented.

Part C: Machinery for working out new
development targets

Examples of administrative arrangements for
the participation of ministries of labour
and employers' and workers' organisations
in development planning

In Australia the Minister for Labour and Immigration is
responsible for the formulation of policy and the provision of
information and advice to the Commonwealth Government on labour
and manpower matters. At the very highest level, labour and
manpower policies are reviewed and co-ordinated with other
economic and social objectives by the central Cabinet, of which
the Minister for Labour and Immigration is a member. Below
cabinet level there is an extremely widespread network of formal
and informal arrangements for consultation with other departments,
outside organisations and individuals who represent the interests
and viewpoints of all elements of society. Although there are
no statutory rules concerning the participation of employers and
workers in the development of new targets, it is a well-
established practice of the Commonwealth and States' Governments
to work with consultative and advisory bodies which include among
their members representatives of employers' and workers' organisations, for instance on the annual pre-budget discussions of the
Department of Labour and Immigration.

In Bangladesh the Ministry of Labour and Social Welfare
participates in the preparation of five-year economic plans by
the National Planning Commission. Targets of industrial production are arrived at through consultation between different
ministries, including the Ministry of Labour and Social Welfare.
Such targets are included in the five-year plan and the annual
plan, and are further elaborated in the industrial investment
schedule prepared by the Ministry of Industries with the labour
ministry participating in an advisory capacity. Employers and
workers are also consulted on such target setting.

In Fiji the Development Committee, comprising a standing
committee of the Council of Ministers under the chairmanship of
the Chief Minister, is assisted by a development subcommittee,
composed of the Secretaries to the Ministers on the Development
Committee together with specialist government officers or
representatives of the private sector. The Minister and the
Secretary for Labour are members of the Development Committee
and subcommittee respectively. Technical expertise is provided
by the Central Planning Office, which is part of the Ministry of
Finance. In the field of manpower, the Manpower Resources
Council, comprising official members and members from both sides
of industry, is charged with ensuring that manpower requirements
in both private and public sectors are assessed, and with undertaking periodic reviews of manpower and production priorities.
The Council reports to the Chief Minister and in practice
proposals emanating from the Council are referred to the Development Committee or its subcommittee as may be appropriate. The
Secretary for Labour is deputy chairman of the Manpower Resources
Council. Employers and workers are associated in the development
of new labour policies through the National Labour Advisory Board,
and are also represented on the National Manpower Council.

In India the Planning Commission, which is responsible for the formulation of national development plans (five-year and annual plans), is composed of five independent members, including a full-time deputy chairman. The Prime Minister is Chairman of the Commission and the Finance Minister is an ex officio member. One member is responsible for the labour aspects of the plan. Within the machinery of the Planning Commission itself, there is a unit called the Labour and Employment Division, whose responsibility it is to process the programmes submitted by the Central Department of Labour and Employment (within the Ministry of Labour and Rehabilitation) as well as by the state labour departments, and also to advise the member in charge of labour on labour and employment policies. The Planning Unit in the Department of Labour and Employment works closely with the Labour and Employment Division of the Planning Commission. The Ministry of Labour is associated in the labour panels and working groups set up by the Planning Commission during the preparation of the plan. The plan contains a specific chapter on employment, manpower and labour welfare. Employers and workers are indirectly associated with the planning process through the major advisory bodies in which they are represented.

In Indonesia the National Planning Body (BAPPENAS) is entrusted with the drawing up, evaluation and supervision of the plan, which is carried out through programmes and projects. The Department of Manpower, Transmigration and Co-operatives supports BAPPENAS in making an assessment of the manpower implications of the national plan. It furthermore executes development projects covering vocational training, management training, government staff training, productivity studies and improvement of productivity, workers' education, labour-intensive systems, etc. Employers and workers are also encouraged to participate in the development of new development targets.

In Japan the Ministry of Labour participates in the formulation of economic and social development plans such as the Basic Economic and Social Development Plan and the National Over-all Development Plan by submitting its opinions on the drafts of such plans to the Economic Planning Agency. The Economic Planning Agency is the government agency responsible for the formulation of such plans. In this country, in line with the plans already mentioned in this report, the Ministry of Labour itself develops a series of plans and programmes. Some of the major plans and programmes are: (i) the Second Basic Employment Measures Plan (1972-76) which was drawn up after consultation with heads of administrative agencies, prefectural governors and the tripartite Employment Deliberation Council; (ii) the Prefectural Basic Employment Plans drawn up in line with the main plan; (iii) the National and Prefectural Annual Employment Programmes for implementation of the plan; (iv) the Basic Vocational Training Plan; (v) the Industrial Accident Prevention Programme; (vi) the Labour Standards Administration Programme; and (vii) the Basic Policy for Measures to Promote Working Women's Welfare.

The draft plans are discussed at the Vice-Ministers' meeting and at the Cabinet meeting before their formal approval by the Cabinet. The Vice-Minister for Labour and the Minister for Labour participate respectively in the discussion and in the adoption of such plans. Whenever concrete policy measures are to be formulated on the basis of such plans (e.g. drafting of relevant bills for enactment of laws and regulations) by the government departments in their respective sphere of competence, the labour ministry is consulted in the preparatory stage of drafting and thus participates in the formulation of such policy measures. Employers' and workers' representatives actively participate in the establishment of these economic and social development plans, for instance through their membership of the Economic Deliberation Council, which submits its opinion to the Prime Minister, at his request, concerning these plans.

In Malaysia the Economic Planning Unit (EPU) of the Prime Minister's Department has the over-all jurisdiction for manpower planning matters. The Ministry of Labour and Manpower has considerably enhanced its competence and capability in this field since the establishment of the Manpower Department of the Ministry. Close working relations are now maintained between the EPU and the Ministry of Labour and Manpower with respect to plan preparation in the fields of labour, manpower and employment. The views of workers and employers are sought through the various advisory bodies to the Ministry of Labour and through representation in the EPU.

In Mongolia the trade unions actively participate on an equal footing with other institutions in working out measures concerning the formulation of future development plans.

In New Zealand the National Plan consists of a series of targets or guiding principles adopted by the National Development Conference. The treatment given to labour and manpower in the National Plan consists of a series of recommendations of the Labour Committee of the National Development Conference which approves them. The agency responsible for establishing the plan is the National Development Council. The Department of Labour is represented in each of the sectoral councils which are established in the National Development Council for each sector of the economy. The Research and Planning Division of the Department of Labour is in day-to-day contact with the Secretariat of the Council. The views of employers and workers are sought on major items of government labour policy.

In Pakistan the Planning Commission within the President's Secretariat has the over-all responsibility for drawing up the National Plan. The President is the chairman of the Commission and the deputy chairman with ministerial status ex officio has been made operational head of the Commission. The Planning Commission, while preparing the fourth five-year plan (1970-75) appointed 23 advisory panels on different subjects consisting of officials drawn from the central and the provincial governments and non-official experts in order to facilitate the work of formulating the plan. The representatives of the Ministry of Labour and Works were associated with the following three panels: (i) manpower; (ii) social welfare; and (iii) management and productivity. Employers' and workers' organisations are associated, through the Tripartite Labour Conference and the Standing Labour Committee, with the formulation of governmental labour policies.

In the Philippines the National Manpower and Youth Council, which is attached to the Department of Labour for policy and programme co-ordination, has the responsibility for formulating a long-term national manpower plan for the optimum allocation, development and utilisation of manpower for employment, entrepreneurship and social and economic growth. This manpower plan has, after its adoption by the Council, to be updated annually and submitted to the President for his approval. After the President's approval, the manpower plan is the controlling plan for the development of manpower resources in the entire country in accordance with the National Development Plan. The National Manpower and Youth Council has a tripartite structure. On the government side, the chairman is, ex officio, the Secretary of Labour, while the Secretary of Education and Culture is, ex officio, vice-chairman, and as ex officio members there are the Director-General of the National Economic and Development Authority, the Secretary of Agriculture and Natural Resources, the Secretary of Industries, the Secretary of Social Welfare, the Secretary of Local Governments and Community Development, the Chairman of the National Science Development Board and the Executive Director of the Council.

In this country the Secretary of Labour as well as the Secretary for Education have recently become regular members of the National Economic and Development Authority, which is the agency responsible for preparing the over-all National Development Plan.

In Sri Lanka the National Planning Council, which has the over-all responsibility for drawing up the National Development Plan, has established a series of sectoral committees which are advisory bodies to the Council. Staff of the Ministry of Planning and Economic Affairs form the secretariat of these committees. The Ministry of Labour is usually consulted on all new targets in the field of labour to be set in the national plans and the views of the Ministry are duly taken into consideration. The setting of targets in the field of employment and manpower is the responsibility of the Ministry of Planning and Economic Affairs.

In Thailand the Department of Labour contributes to the preparation of the national development plans by submission of proposals approved by the Minister of the Interior (responsible for labour affairs) to the National Economic and Social Development Board.

The approach to participation is different in the USSR, where the Central Council of Trade Unions co-operates with the State Planning Commission, and the plan documents concerned with social matters need the approval by that Council prior to submission to the Supreme Soviet. The members of the Central Council of Trade Unions are ex officio members of the Prices Committee of the State Planning Commission, as well as of other functional committees set up by the Government.

CHAPTER II

SOME PROBLEMS AND POSSIBLE SOLUTIONS

In the preceding chapter an effort was made to describe the role which Asian labour ministries are playing in the various areas of national development and to illustrate, by way of example, the variety of activities which they are carrying out at the moment as well as the ways and means by which employers' and workers' organisa tions are associated with these activities. It is against this background that the need for strengthening labour administration in Asia must be viewed, a need which is so widespread and generally fel that the 16th Session of the Asian Advisory Committee proposed, and the Governing Body approved, placing the present item on the agenda of the Eighth Asian Regional Conference.

In putting the emphasis on strengthening labour administration in Asia, on enhancing the role of labour ministries in national development and on promoting the active participation of employers' and workers' organisations in labour administration activities, the present chapter attempts to spell out a number of problem areas and to raise a number of suggestions which the Conference may wish to discuss. After considering general aspects of the scope of res- ponsibility of labour administration in Asia, this chapter will briefly discuss possible new scope for labour administration activities in the three major areas described above, i.e. employment and training; income and conditions of work and life; and labour relations. This will be followed by a consideration of means of achieving more effective participation by employers' and workers' organisations, and of measures that may be taken to increase the administrative efficiency of labour ministries. The final section reviews briefly present and possible future measures at the inter- national level.

Part A: **Problems related to the scope**
         of responsibility of ministries
         of labour

 Influences determining the scope of the responsibility entruste to the labour ministries include the financial situation of the government and the allocation of priorities in the process of national development. In some countries, such priorities initially placed heavy emphasis on economic aspects. The need for a better balance between economic and social development - stressed in the United Nations Strategy for the Second Development Decade - has more recently been given wider acceptance.

At present, however, there is a considerable amount of debate in various countries and also at the international level over the desirability of reviewing the scope of responsibility of such ministries. This debate is due on the one hand to an appreciation of the need to reassess the expected value of the contribution of labour ministries to national development, and on the other hand, to these ministries' success in demonstrating their capacity to con- tribute effectively to achieving objectives of national development policy. In many countries, the ministry of labour does not rank sufficiently high among the agencies of government and may con- sequently have been bypassed at higher levels of decision making.

In some cases, labour ministries have, in fact, found it difficult to cope effectively with the full range of new problems arising from rapidly changing conditions in their countries.

Population growth, pressure on land resources, urbanisation and relatively slow rates of economic expansion have created tremendous imbalances between job demand and supply in some countries. Under-employment and the imbalance of income levels between various groups of the national workforce (including rural labour) have in certain cases reached dramatic proportions. Furthermore, both these types of imbalances have been growing in a number of countries at an accelerated pace due to recent energy problems and inflationary trends. The fall in prices of certain commodities and consequent worsening in the terms of trade of certain countries have further aggravated the situation.

Faced with these and other short-term or structural problems, several Asian ministries of labour have responded by trying to improve and expand their services dealing with employment, training and income questions. While their range of responsibility may also have expanded to some extent, this has not always been the case. But there is more widespread recognition than in the past that a labour ministry's functions are not necessarily limited to the traditional responsibilities of employment exchange operation, promotion of apprenticeship and industrial skills training, better enforcement of statutory minimum wages and working conditions or settlement of labour disputes. As a matter of fact, many labour ministries are already facing up to the magnitude and gravity of the burning new problems arising from rapid national development.

Small wonder, therefore, that officials in Asian labour ministries as well as employers' and workers' representatives are increasingly concerned about what labour ministries are doing and could be doing in the various problem areas concerned. They ask such questions as: has the responsibility of Asian labour ministries grown quantitatively and qualitatively in such matters as information gathering and research work; contribution to the development planning process in government; plan and programme implementation, fostering of institutional arrangements for securing the participation of employers' and workers' organisations in relevant aspects of labour administration; more effective administration of labour affairs for the national workforce as a whole through provision of better field services; more attention to the problems of labour in agriculture, the rural areas and small enterprises; increased attention to the employment problems of women and young persons; playing a meaningful role towards under-utilised sectors of the labour force, such as the unemployed and underemployed; and so forth.

Needless to say, such major issues as the imbalances in the labour market and in the income levels of a country are the res-ponsibility of the government as a whole and hence numerous ministries and public agencies of the national administration have a part to play in dealing with such problems. Furthermore, many of the problems concerned are - depending on the general set-up of the country concerned - not a matter for government intervention but must be tackled by non-governmental organisations, primarily those representing employers and workers. Thus the establishment of new services or the expansion of existing services of the labour ministry - however important it may be - can only provide a partial answer to the problems concerned and can only be seen as a part of the over-all policy measures required.

The search for solutions to national development problems in many Asian countries has so far brought about more tangible success in fields like health administration, general education, building of physical infrastructure and increased food supplies than in the fields with which labour administration is more directly concerned. It is not sufficient to rely on development plans to reduce the imbalances in employment and incomes. Of equal importance is the need to take measures of a practical nature, by way of governmental or tripartite arrangements, to counteract these imbalances as and when they occur or before they further deteriorate. From this point of view also, it is important to widen the range of responsibilities entrusted to labour ministries and to promote the participation of employers' and workers' organisations.

At the time of drafting and adopting national development plans, which are usually established for a period of several years, it is impossible to take account of all the factors which might influence future changes in the employment and income situation. Moreover, there are always unforeseeable developments such as fluctuations in prices and exchange rates, demand fluctuations and changes in investment and commodity stock levels, not to speak of unpredictable climatic disturbances or political developments.

The main problems concerning the strengthening of labour ministries in Asia and the widening of their scope of responsibility are related to such questions as:

- How can labour ministries be equipped better to appreciate the need for the attainment both of economic goals and of the objectives of social justice and a fairer sharing of the national wealth, without which the living standards and productive capacity of the labour force - and thereby those of the general population - will not be raised?

- How can the role assigned to labour ministries be enhanced with a consequent increase of operating resources for such ministries?

- How can labour ministries be allocated a wider range of responsibilities concerning the population in the rural areas, which forms the largest proportion of the manpower in many Asian countries, and concerning the promotion of employment in small-scale industry and the informal sector?

- How can labour ministries be integrated into the governmental processes of development planning and programme implementation?

- How can institutional arrangements be made or improved for associating organisations of employers and workers with the administration of public affairs, particularly in the field of economic and social development?

- How can the dispersal of labour administration functions over a number of public departments, including parastatal agencies under the supervision of other ministries, be avoided?

- How can institutional arrangements be made for the co-ordination of policy making and execution in regard to labour administration?

- How can the labour ministry be developed so as to be in a
  position to exercise general responsibility for helping to
  achieve coherence and effective application of government
  policy in the labour field?

Part B: Problems in providing employment
         and training services

The provision of employment services is usually the exclusive
responsibility of labour ministries, although measures for employment promotion and for increased over-all utilisation of the national
workforce depend, as far as government measures are concerned,
largely on decisions by ministries of finance, industry and commerce,
agriculture, transport, etc., and by the government as a whole in
the context of its general strategy for employment, education and
manpower development. Nevertheless, in certain Asian countries,
the ministry of labour has a fairly substantial role in formulating
policies for promoting manpower demand in the organised sector,
while the implementation of these policies is mainly the responsibility of other agencies. Instead, the ministry of labour plays a
large role in both the formulation and the implementation of policies
affecting the supply of labour.

However, even with regard to the more technical and traditional
aspects of manpower skill development, for which the labour ministry
may have a fairly wide competence, for example vocational training
(including management development and certain schemes of training
for rural workers), its mandate is sometimes confined to the
promotion and supervision of apprenticeship and other forms of in-
service or on-the-job training for industrial workers. Training
centres for craftsmen and other skilled workers may be under the
ministries of education or of industry and commerce.

The following paragraphs discuss some of the more specific
problems and difficulties which have a bearing on the provision of
governmental services in the field of employment and manpower
development.

Employment

One basic need in this field is the assembly and analysis of
employment information, the conduct of manpower surveys and the use
of prospective studies and forecasting in regard to future employment and manpower trends in the country's economy.

With regard to employment information, the problem in some
Asian countries seems to be partly one of co-ordination between
ministries of labour and other governmental agencies and partly one
of internal constraints.

On the one hand, there is a need for detailed information, and
on the other hand, there are limited resources for information
collection. In order to be of practical use, such information must
cover the types, the extent and the changes in trend of the
imbalances between job supply and job demand. These imbalances
are the result of the interaction of various factors, including the
fact that industrial expansion and agricultural development or
services do not adequately absorb the net increase of the labour
force and the rates of absorption of men and women workers into

employment do not correspond to the degree of willingness to work of the two sexes. An imbalance often exists between educational qualifications and job requirements, in that persons possessing the appropriate qualifications and skills are not available while, on the other hand, the education system continues to turn out people for whose skills there is no foreseeable demand. Structural change in the economy render many people unemployed who then need retraining or further training and the mobility of labour may not be adjusted as between areas of labour surplus and areas of growing or new demand for labour.

Another problem area in the operation of employment services is their geographical coverage. Relatively few countries in Asia have a widespread system of employment information offices and exchanges.

Other problems affecting the working of employment market information include communication difficulties, maldistribution of employment offices, the fact that small-scale industry and the often large "informal" sector of both urban and rural employment is overlooked, difficulties in the widespread use of standard occupational classifications, and the inability or unwillingness of some enterprises to assist the authorities adequately in the assembly of this type of information.

Moreover, in some countries the concepts of employment, unemployment and underemployment are not clearly defined. Definition used in North America or Europe do not suit the needs of Asia. There are also large information gaps in a number of countries with regard to the employment situation and changes in employment levels in the rural sector. Furthermore, the connection between levels of employment and income throughout the economy needs further study. Labour ministries could do much more to intensify their activities in the field of labour mobility, transmigration between various regions, and population questions.

Problems arise also from the time factor in the working of employment services. Too much delay in the collection of employment information can make this function a practically useless exercise. It is unavoidable that the results of population censuses can only be made available after long delays - often two or three years. Because of these delays and because censuses provide only structural information, many Asian countries have developed systems of employment market information which produce the data more frequently (every one or two months, with summaries every one or two years) and more rapid systems of data analysis have been established, as under the computer-based systems in Japan and Malaysia.

One of the factors which create obstacles to the running of an efficient employment market information system in some Asian countries is the dispersal of responsibility for such data collection over various government agencies. This may result in duplication of work. Obviously, there is no need for employment services to try to provide information which is made available by other agencies. For instance, national census bureaus provide important information concerning the main structural changes in the labour force; national bureaux of statistics usually provide information on the general level of employment and its breakdown by industry, sex and age; and ministries of finance, mines, industries education, etc. collect some associated relevant information derived from their normal work.

In a number of countries, there is co-ordination of the employment information function through national manpower councils or
commissions, in which the various government agencies concerned are
represented along with organisations of employers and of workers.
Ministries of labour could assist in this co-ordination by working
out guidelines for an over-all system of the collection of data
relevant to employment.

Other institutional problems concern the numbers, quality and
training of the staff of the employment services, the availability
of equipment and data processing machinery, and the degree of co-
operation obtained from other government departments and from
organisations of employers and workers, for instance, through the
use of tripartite committees at regional and local levels in
support of the work of the employment service.

With regard to certain Asian countries where mass unemployment
and underemployment is a central problem, the question could be
asked whether it should really be a primary function of labour
administration to focus its attention on the registration of job
seekers when less than one in a hundred of them has a chance of
being placed in a job through the assistance of the employment
service of the labour ministry.   In such a situation, it might be
preferable to concentrate the work of labour administration more on
assistance to over-all employment promotion efforts within the
framework of general policies, more rapid collection of employment
market data, more widespread programmes of vocational orientation,
career guidance, measures to offset excessive urbanisation, specific
measures of manpower adjustment, etc.

With regard to employment promotion, several ministries of
labour in Asia have problems in identifying their specific role.
Due to institutional, personnel and financial restraints, a number
of these ministries are at present not in a position to perform a
very active role in this area.   But there are exceptions.   Some
ministries of labour are preparing annual and rolling employment
plans in line with the national plan, while, for instance, the
Australian Department of Labour and Immigration has been reorganised
recently and has been given substantially increased budgetary
resources to permit greater attention to be given to problems of
employment promotion and vocational training.   Research activities
have also been strengthened, as well as internal management in the
Department and staff-training arrangements.

Training, retraining and rehabilitation

The imbalance between the skills possessed by job seekers and
the skills needed in the process of national development is one of
the major problems for several countries in Asia.   In many cases,
the problem creates immense difficulties for ministries of labour
and educational authorities due to the great number of people
involved and the inadequacies in quantity or quality of the human
resources development services.   As mentioned above, part of the
function of promoting measures for skill development is usually
attributed to the labour ministry and the actual provision and
operation of vocational training centres may be partly this
ministry's responsibility and partly that of other agencies.
Practice in this respect differs considerably between countries of
the region.   At the administrative level, one of the problems may
be the distribution of responsibilities in this field in Asian

countries. For instance, the need is sometimes felt for clear distinctions between responsibilities for technical and vocational education of youth within the general school system, apprenticeship and other in-plant training for young persons, pre-employment training in technical training institutions outside the school system, and the training of adults including retraining through various schemes. Examples quoted in the previous chapter indicate that special bodies have sometimes had to be established to co-ordinate the activities of educational, labour administration and other agencies - distinguishing for instance between over-all national standard setting and control, provision for individual industries, and provision for assistance to undertakings and government departments in carrying out their role in planning. A fairly common role of labour administration has been to foster and supervise apprenticeship training and other forms of in-plant and in-service training. Sometimes, however, the employment and training services of the government have insufficient resources to carry out effective promotional work in the field of training and to supervise the results of in-service training. Some countries have imposed legal obligations on employers to provide training or have established systems of training levies so as to finance collective schemes.

To the extent to which Asian labour ministries have assumed responsibility in the field of training, the main practical problems facing them may be summarised as including the following questions:

- how to ensure, by means of participation in appropriate institutions, the co-ordination of the activities of agencies responsible respectively in the fields of education and labour administration and in other fields together with the representation of the views of employers' and workers' organisations in this regard;

- how to establish a sufficient number of vocational training institutes, with sufficient input and output of trainees and appropriate numbers and quality of instructors;

- how to organise apprenticeship and in-plant training on a sufficient scale and related in a practical way to the institutional training schemes;

- how to cater better for the rural labour force in the context of rural development and improved production of food supply;

- how to provide the right incentives for further acquisition of skills and to ensure their utilisation through appropriate career development arrangements;

- how to improve labour mobility and job security by sufficient provision for retraining of workers whose jobs or particular skills are becoming redundant;

- how to adjust the educational system and pre-vocational preparation measures so that they match the demand for skills better and do not produce candidates for job opportunities which are limited or liable to decline;

- how best to assist in controlling the quality of vocational training and vocational education.

While some of the ministries of labour in Asia have services which are sufficiently developed to deal fairly effectively with the above matters, others have inadequate resources and staff.

Here again, institutional arrangements for securing the co-operation of organisations of employers and of workers need to be further developed. While most countries have provided the basic tripartite or bipartite machinery in this respect, it is sometimes not as actively used as it could be.

Part C: Problems related to income and conditions of work and life

Inseparable from the employment problem is the income problem. The basic question for a large number of Asian countries has been - and still is - how to help in creating the conditions which ensure full, freely chosen and productive employment for all workers with commensurate, adequate levels of income.

The conclusion of the Fourth Asian Labour Ministers' Conference (1973) indicated that "poverty, unemployment and underemployment are the most serious problems and that unemployment was the greatest exploiter of labour and the greatest threat to peace and prosperity".[1]

As regards income, labour ministries could play a central role by collecting and analysing information on wages paid, cost of living development and indices, and other matters relating to workers' incomes, and could make this information available to other government agencies, especially those in charge of working out national development plans.

Traditionally, Asian labour ministries have been more directly involved in the industrialised sectors of the economy as well as in the services and plantations sectors, which face particular problems with regard to wages and other conditions of work.

In several countries the machinery for the fixing of minimum wages is inadequate, as is the machinery for the enforcement of minimum wage rates. This problem is particularly sharp where the number of inspectors is insufficient in comparison to the number of workers covered by the minimum wage legislation. It also concerns the ability of the inspectors effectively to check the wages paid in the enterprises involved, particularly handicraft and small-scale enterprises in the rural areas. Clearly, the problems of the labour inspectorates are aggravated in some Asian countries by the relative weakness of the trade unions.

A central problem in several Asian countries is the very low standard of working conditions, especially in the medium and small-size undertakings which often completely escape the attention of the labour inspectorate, due to the latter's inadequate staff and resources, or to the former's very weak economic position, making it difficult for small enterprises to comply with the prescribed minimum pay rates and generally with the existing labour legislation. This problem often becomes particularly serious as regards the employment of women and children, and in the field of occupational safety and health generally.

---

[1] Fourth Asian Labour Ministers' Conference (Tokyo, 1973), Joint Communiqué, para. 7.

As regards protection against occupational hazards, in several countries problems arise from rapid industrialisation, which has out paced the expansion of the inspectorate. The expansion and diversification of industry and continuous technological evolution have left behind labour inspectorates in several countries, where such inspectorates have not been able to acquire the new technical competence or the means and resources to investigate all such workplaces. A high rate of occupational accidents and diseases has been noted in certain cases. Particularly the poorer countries cannot afford the technical backing of labour inspectors by research and educational institutes which would be required to make inspectio more effective. But international assistance could be considered in this field. In some countries, the quality of the work of the labour inspectorate has suffered from the growing volume of work and the multiplicity of the legislation subject to enforcement by labour inspectors, or from the dispersal of functions among various branche of inspection.

In many Asian countries labour ministries have found it impossible to establish - let alone enforce - minimum income levels or working conditions for the rural workers outside plantations. In some cases, however, as in India, the ministry of labour has made a beginning on defining and promoting a minimum level of income for agricultural labourers. This income level is expressed in terms of "money equivalent" of a basket of food, education, housing, health care and freedom from social disabilities. While problems do still occur, the ministry is promoting the creation of agencies at the village level for augmenting the bargaining power of this section of the labour force.

Government measures which aim at raising incomes in rural sectors are sometimes taken, with or without the assistance of the ministry of labour, but the question concerning the latter's long-term contribution in this domain remains largely unsolved. A more active involvement of labour ministries in these measures would clearly be desirable, especially as regards programmes relating to rural public works, the promotion of consumer and production co-operatives, promotion of rural workers' organisations, special youth programmes, and programmes for the educated unemployed. The major problems with regard to such activities are limitations in funds and administrative resources (from the ministerial to the village level) which would be necessary to plan and carry out these activities on a sufficiently vast scale.

The whole question of long-term social security for the rural workers remains unsolved in many Asian countries mainly due to financial constraints, a problem which goes far beyond the mere question of the capabilities of labour administration agencies. Workers' housing is another problem area in which some Asian labour ministries are assuming increased responsibilities, and others could follow this path.

Part D: <u>Problems related to the administration of labour relations</u>

The role of the government, and particularly of the labour ministry, in the field of labour relations has on several occasions been discussed by the Asian Regional Conference in the past. For instance, the Fifth Asian Regional Conference (Melbourne, 1962) discussed the subject "Government services for the improvement of

labour management relations and settlement of disputes" and the
Seventh Asian Regional Conference (Teheran, 1971) debated, under the
agenda item on "Freedom of association of workers' and employers'
organisations and their role in social and economic development", a
whole range of labour relations issues and the labour ministries'
role in this regard.   It is therefore not considered necessary to
raise in the present report all the problems and suggestions discussed in the past with regard to the strengthening of the labour
relations services of Asian ministries of labour.   Clearly, most of
the suggestions formulated at previous sessions of the Asian
Regional Conference have kept all their validity.

For instance, one of these suggestions concerns the building up
of an effective conciliation service, through appointing a permanent
specialised conciliation staff, through better recruitment procedures
and conditions, through a better and more systematic staff development programme, through appropriate backing up of the conciliation
service by studies and research at headquarter levels, and through
the issue of guidelines to conciliators.   Another suggestion made
in the past which has remained valid for some Asian ministries of
labour concerns the appointment of arbitrators for voluntary
arbitration.   With regard to compulsory arbitration, unfair labour
practices and trade union recognition or workers' representation for
purposes of collective bargaining, much could be done in many Asian
countries to improve the functioning of the labour ministries'
agencies dealing with these problems.   Other still valid suggestions
include the role of labour ministries in promoting collective bargaining, both through more extensive educational work to employers
and workers and through encouragement and assistance in the forma-
tion and functioning of collective bargaining machinery.

One central issue in the area of labour relations is the working out of a national labour relations policy which was recommended
by the Seventh Asian Regional Conference and for which that
conference formulated a series of guidelines and principles.
Clearly, the initiative for the development of such a policy will
in most cases have to lie with the labour ministry, in close
association with the employers' and workers' organisations concerned.

Part E: Participation by employers' and workers'
         organisations in Asian labour administration

Many times reference has been made to the need for more active
participation by employers' and workers' organisations in the
functioning of national systems of labour administration.   The
closer these organisations are associated with solving labour, manpower, employment and income problems, the easier it will be for the
ministry of labour to carry out its functions.

With respect to labour policy and general target setting for
the activities of the ministry of labour, it is desirable that
employers' and workers' organisations be effectively consulted either
on an ad hoc basis or through existing institutions such as a
national labour advisory council, provided that the latter are
effectively and regularly convened and their advice is taken into
account.

With respect to employment and training services, both
employers' and workers' organisations have a great interest in
their effective functioning.   Employers' and workers' organisations

could play an important role as members of national, regional or local employment committees - the latter attached to the regional or local employment service in order to assist the director of such an office in carrying out his functions.

In the training field, tripartite apprenticeship committees, vocational training councils or human resources development committees could make a substantial contribution to the consolidation of in-plant training, apprenticeship training and other forms of informal training into a coherent system of training, adjusted to the needs of the country.

With respect to labour inspection, collaboration between the labour inspectorate and employers' and workers' organisations is a prerequisite for efficient and successful operation. These organisations can also help in setting targets for the inspectorate and supporting the inspectorate in its daily work.

Clearly, these various forms of associating employers' and workers' organisations with the operation of a labour administration system must be considered in the wider context of participation of workers' and employers' organisations in the elaboration and implementation of national development plans. As this matter was discussed by the Seventh Asian Regional Conference, which adopted a detailed resolution on the subject[1], the various aspects of this question are not considered in the present report.

Part F: Effectiveness of the ministry of labour as an administration

In addition to strengthening the services of a ministry of labour through widening the scope of its responsibilities, enhancing its status in the government machine and raising its technical competence and innovative capacity in the various technical fields for which it is directly responsible, and promoting more active participation by employers' and workers' organisations in the work of labour administration agencies, some consideration might also be given to strengthening the operation of Asian labour ministries with regard to their internal organisation.

All Asian ministries of labour pursue certain objectives, but it might be useful to formulate these objectives more explicitly, perhaps in a policy document or in legislation, in co-operation with employers' and workers' organisations. Work programmes as defined already by several Asian ministries of labour may sometimes need further elaboration, and might for instance include targets in the fields of labour inspection, occupational safety and health, employment services, training, conditions of work and life and minimum income levels.

---

[1] Resolution concerning freedom of association for workers' and employers' organisations and their role in social and economic development, Record of proceedings, Seventh Asian Regional Conference (Teheran, December 1971), Geneva, ILO, p. 219.

The staff of Asian ministries of labour constitutes the "back-
bone" of the activities of these ministries. In some cases, it may
be necessary to upgrade and train their staff more extensively.
The Asian Advisory Committee, at its 16th Session (Kuala Lumpur,
1974) concluded in this regard that "the training of labour
administration staff is essential and a continuing requirement,
particularly in the context of the new and expanding responsibilities
of labour ministries. Training programmes should be reviewed from
time to time by the ministry of labour in consultation with the
representatives of the staff and should be improved and upgraded in
accordance with national needs".[1]

The "matching" of functional requirements with skills in labour
administration was discussed by a recent Seminar on Training Needs
for Labour Administrators in Asia (Berlin, Bonn, Geneva, November
1974), organised by the German Foundation for International
Development with the collaboration of the ILO. The report of the
seminar spells out in some detail a number of useful suggestions
which Asian labour ministries may wish to consider with a view to
overcoming the imbalance between the skills needed and the skills
possessed by their staff at various levels. Several types of
training like induction, on-the-job, refresher and management training were discussed, and their respective contents reviewed.
Attention might be given in this regard to the opportunities
afforded to the staff of a ministry of labour not only of performing
routine functions, but also of displaying initiative in the area of
work for which they are responsible. Officially encouraged
improvements in communication through joint meetings or other means
could be considered.

Staff remuneration has remained a problem within several Asian
ministries of labour. Officials who are unable to maintain a
decent standard of living for their families on their salaries cannot be expected to carry out their functions properly. In some
countries, the salary structure in the labour ministry is such that
the best officials do not stay very long in their jobs as they
prefer to accept attractive offers from private employers. A high
staff turnover in labour administration is of course detrimental to
its proper functioning.

The sharing of work between the top and lower echelons has in
some Asian ministries of labour led to overburdening of the senior
officials because not all the staff in the lower echelons have the
qualifications to carry out the responsibilities assigned to them.
It might therefore be advisable to consider increased delegation of
authority to well-trained staff, while through improved systems of
management information the top labour administrators could be kept
up to date with the activities of the ministry. The more the
ministry works according to a programme, the easier it will be to
delegate certain responsibilities to lower levels of the hierarchy.
The top administrators can then concentrate on the thinking and
planning necessary for attaining the targets set.

It seems also that in several Asian countries the co-ordination
of labour administration activities could be improved upon. The
instrument for such co-ordination exists in most Asian countries,
where there is already a central body for labour administration, i.e.

---

[1] Report on the 16th Session of the Asian Advisory Committee
(Kuala Lumpur, May 1974), GB.193/8/16, para. 104.

the ministry of labour or its equivalent. In practically all Asian countries these ministries co-operate closely with regional and local offices or, in federal states, with the state or provincial departments of labour. But the need for co-ordination has differen characteristics in federal countries, in some of which the federal government as well as the state governments has certain legislative and executive powers in labour matters, according to the constitutional distribution of responsibilities. The pursuit of a coherent labour, manpower and employment policy requires an institutional framework, the basis for which exists in most of the countries concerned, and within which the state or provincial labour departments can collaborate with the central ministry of labour.

In unitary countries, the need is rather to prevent the dispersal of labour administration functions among various agencies and to ensure close collaboration between headquarters and field offices This applies especially to employment and training, but also to a large extent to incomes and wages and sharing the fruits of economic growth.

In many Asian countries, labour administration offices in the field perform multi-purpose activities. As it is impossible to ask them to expand all their activities in each specialised area, the need is for better integration of the field structure with programme preparation and implementation, so that there is a greater likelihood of success in attaining specified targets.

Co-ordination between the various services of some Asian labour ministries also requires greater attention. This applies particularly to co-ordination between employment and manpower services and the more traditional labour services (labour inspection and labour relations). The knowledge labour inspectors gain during their visits to undertakings is relevant both to the employment and training services and to the labour relations services, but often this information is not made generally available.

Part G: Present and possible future measures
         at the international level

In the Asian region, a series of activities has been going on in recent years in the field of labour administration with the assistance of the ILO, particularly as regards technical co-operatio As it is of course impossible to list here all the activities of the ILO which have an impact upon labour administration generally, the following remarks are restricted to the ILO's specific activities within its labour administration programme. These activities can be subdivided under three headings:

(i)   exchanges of experience and training;

(ii) expert assistance in various fields of labour administra-
      tion; and

(iii) research and studies.

With regard to exchange of experience, several methods have been used. Participants in workshops, seminars, etc. have greatly contributed to this exchange by explaining to participants from other countries the situation as regards labour administration in their own country and these discussions have greatly helped in keeping Asian labour administration agencies informed about the activities carried out by such agencies in other Asian countries.

The ILO has organised within its labour administration programme:

- with UNDP assistance

1. an Asian Round Table on Labour Administration and Development Planning (Philippines, 1969);

2. the First and Second Asian Regional Labour Policy and Administration Training Courses (Japan, 1971 and Australia, 1972);

3. an Asian Regional Workshop on the Functions and Organisation of Labour Ministry Services Dealing with Employment Questions (India, 1975);

- with Swedish assistance

4. an ILO/SIDA Asian Regional Seminar on Labour Inspection in relation to the Employment of Women and Protection of Children (Singapore, 1972);

- with Japanese assistance

5. an ILO/Japan Asian Regional Workshop for the Exercise of Responsibilities of Labour Departments with regard to Women Workers (Japan, 1974).

The ILO also collaborated in a Seminar on the Training Needs for Labour Administrators in Asia (Federal Republic of Germany, 1974), organised by the German Foundation for International Development.

Within the context of the Asian Regional Project for Strengthening Labour and Manpower Administration (ARPLA), experts from this project participated in country training programmes in Bangladesh, Indonesia, Sri Lanka and Thailand, while their participation is anticipated for several more countries.

In the context of the same project, fellows from various Asian labour administration agencies were received by the New Zealand Department of Labour for a study-cum-observation tour. The exchange of experience was facilitated by ARPLA consultants who had carried out country missions to study and advise on the labour administration system in various countries.

Expert assistance was also provided through national projects in Indonesia, Iran, Khmer Republic, Laos, Nepal, Thailand, the Republic of Viet-Nam and Western Samoa.

Several research studies are being undertaken under ARPLA arrangements. One has been finalised on the "Responsibilities and functions of Asian labour ministries in the formulation and implementation of a national manpower and employment policy and the manner in which such role and functional involvement could be strengthened". This study served as the background paper for a workshop held in New Delhi in May 1975.

Another topic of study which is being undertaken by the same project concerns the "Responsibilities and functions of Asian labour ministries with regard to improving the conditions of work and life of rural and agricultural workers and the possibilities for developing such functions and responsibilities".

Possible future programmes for widening technical co-operation in labour administration may include an extension for a new period of ARPLA, whose first phase will come to an end by December 1975. Other future projects may include the establishment of a sub-regional labour administration project for the South Pacific and studies of and training in national labour market administration.

The exchange of experience could further be widened in several ways. A first possibility would be to arrange under a possible extended ARPLA for the exchange of high-level officials among Asian countries, for periods to be determined with the departments concerned, for observation and/or consultation on matters and problems of immediate interest. This exchange of high-level officials could possibly be arranged among all Asian countries which are willing to support it. The topics for consultation could include such subjects as employment or training administration, the drafting or implementation of labour legislation, etc. The project might assist the requesting country either by helping it to send one of its officials to another Asian country, or by assisting a senior official of another Asian country to travel to the requesting country.

At the senior level, the exchange of experience could further be facilitated by organising, possibly with ARPLA assistance, more regional and subregional seminars and workshops. This would help to widen the outlook and enhance the technical expertise of many officials. Furthermore, visits by some of these officials could be arranged to study certain aspects of labour administration in one or more Asian countries which have a labour administration system with special experience. It would be useful if employers' and workers' organisations could participate in these exchanges of experience.

At the more junior level, there is a need for a combination of on the job training and formal induction training. ARPLA as well as national projects could assist in the formulation as well as the execution of some of these training programmes.

ARPLA could also become the focal point for requests from Asian labour ministries for information on the situation in other Asian countries.

Furthermore, existing staff training manuals, work programmes, etc. used in various Asian labour administration agencies could be brought to the attention of those interested in them. ARPLA could arrange for adjusting such manuals to the conditions of other countries, subject to financial resources. With regard to on-going research in labour administration institutes operating in certain Asian countries (including studies concerned with employment or manpower administration, labour relations administration, occupational safety and health administration, labour inspection, etc.), ARPLA could assist Asian labour ministries to exchange information on the results of such research. For instance, the benefit which some Asian labour inspectorates receive from research made at safety and health institutes in their countries could also be communicated to other Asian countries.

With regard to employment and manpower administration, consideration might, for instance, be given to assisting Asian governments in drawing up annual and rolling employment plans or in establishing employment targets as well as in setting up an effective employment market information system, and a plan of action to be undertaken by ministries of labour in the framework of overall employment policies. Assistance might also be required in connection with the establishment or functioning of national manpower councils, national employment committees, etc. and the definition of their functions.

Suggested list of points for discussion

It has been thought useful to set out below a certain number of points on which the conference may wish to have a discussion. It will, of course, be for the conference to determine whether it wishes to consider all or some of the suggested points or whether there are other points it would wish to discuss.

Strengthening of labour administration in Asia and its role in national development

1. (a) Do the responsibilities of labour administration agencies in Asia need to be redefined with a view to making these agencies more effective instruments of social and economic progress in national development?

   (b) Is there a need to provide, in particular, for greater labour ministry participation in the governmental process of development planning and programme implementation?

2. (a) Is the present degree of participation by employers' and workers' organisations adequate for the "role" desired for labour administration in national development?

   (b) Can this participation be improved?   How?

Employment and training

3. Should labour administration agencies, in Asia, develop their employment information systems more widely so that they cover the periodical measurement of imbalances in job supply and demand with regard to skills, industry, age, sex, education, area and race?

4. Should such agencies in Asia develop annual and rolling employment and manpower plans, or employment and manpower targets, in line with the national development plan and in co-operation with other government agencies and representatives of employers' and workers' organisations?

5. (a) How could Asian ministries of labour, in particular, be equipped to assist in promoting, sponsoring or undertaking activities, in co-operation with employers' and workers' organisations and with other administrations, with a view to enhancing employment opportunities?

   (b) Are new institutional measures needed, such as the establishment of tripartite employment boards attached to labour ministries, or are existing boards or councils in this field adequate?

Income and conditions of work and life

6. Do Asian labour ministries need to review, strengthen or improve their services dealing with matters relating to income and its distribution among various groups, including the rural labour force?

7. Is there a need for special measures to improve the effectiveness of labour inspectorates with regard to the preventive
function in occupational safety and health?

Labour relations

8. Are there improvements which could be made in the consultation
of employers' and workers' organisations on the formulation of
legislative provisions or administrative arrangements for the
functioning of services in this field?

9. How could labour administration agencies assist more effectively
in the promotion of sound labour relations, including collective
bargaining, and in the prevention and settlement of disputes?

Staff and resources

10. Is it desirable to take measures to ensure that the role and
functions of labour administration agencies are more clearly
recognised by other governmental agencies, including the
planning agency, so that a higher share in the national budget
and more staff resources are obtained? What measures could
be taken to this end?

11. Should staff training for labour administration officials be
put on a permanent footing and be made an instrument of change,
so that Asian labour administration agencies become more
capable of responding to the changing needs of their countries?

12. Is it desirable to increase the specialisation of officers like
labour inspectors, labour relations officers and employment
service officers, when local circumstances permit?

Further institutional arrangements for wider participation by employers' and workers' organisations in the functioning of labour administration in Asia

13. Are further institutional measures needed to associate
employers' and workers' organisations more closely with respect
to the implementation of objectives and work programmes in such
fields as:

   - application of labour standards;

   - participation in labour inspection;

   - prevention of occupational safety and health risks;

   - employment, training and vocational orientation programmes;

   - social security programmes?

International technical co-operation

14. What measures could be taken at international level to
strengthen labour administration in Asia with the active
participation of employers' and workers' organisations?

ISBN 92-2-101389
Price: 15 Swiss fran